TEACHER'S GUIDE

daybook, *n.* a book in which the events of the day are recorded; *specif.* a journal or diary

DAYBOOK
of Critical Reading and Writing

GRADE 11

FRAN CLAGGETT

LOUANN REID

RUTH VINZ

Great Source Education Group
a Houghton Mifflin Company
Wilmington, Massachusetts

www.greatsource.com

A u t h o r s

Fran Claggett, currently an educational consultant for schools throughout the country and teacher at Sonoma State University, taught high school English for more than thirty years. She is author of several books, including *Drawing Your Own Conclusions: Graphic Strategies for Reading, Writing, and Thinking* (1992) and *A Measure of Success* (1996).

Louann Reid taught junior and senior high school English, speech, and drama for nineteen years and currently teaches courses for future English teachers at Colorado State University. Author of numerous articles and chapters, her first books were *Learning the Landscape* and *Recasting the Text* with Fran Claggett and Ruth Vinz (1996).

Ruth Vinz, currently a professor and director of English education at Teachers College, Columbia University, taught in secondary schools for twenty-three years. She is author of several books and numerous articles that discuss teaching and learning in the English classroom as well as a frequent presenter, consultant, and co-teacher in schools throughout the country.

Printed in the United States of America

International Standard Book Number: 0-669-46438-4

2 3 4 5 6 7 8 9 10 -POO- 04 03 02 01 00 99

Great Source wishes to acknowledge the many insights and improvements made to the *Daybooks* thanks to the work of the following teachers and educators.

Readers

Jay Amberg
Glenbrook South High School
Glenview, Illinois

Joanne Arellanes
Rancho Cordova, California

Nancy Bass
Moore Middle School
Arvada, Colorado

Jim Benny
Sierra Mountain Middle School
Truckee, California

Noreen Benton
Guilderland High School
Altamont, New York

Janet Bertucci
Hawthorne Junior High School
Vernon Hills, Illinois

Jim Burke
Burlingame High School
Burlingame, California

Mary Castellano
Hawthorne Junior High School
Vernon Hills, Illinois

Diego Davalos
Chula Vista High School
Chula Vista, California

Jane Detgen
Daniel Wright Middle School
Lake Forest, Illinois

Michelle Ditzian
Shepard Junior High School
Deerfield, Illinois

Jenni Dunlap
Highland Middle School
Libertyville, Illinois

Judy Elman
Highland Park High School
Highland Park, Illinois

Mary Ann Evans-Patrick
Fox Valley Writing Project
Oshkosh, Wisconsin

Howard Frishman
Twin Grove Junior High School
Buffalo Grove, Illinois

Kathleen Gaynor
Wheaton, Illinois

Beatrice Gerrish
Bell Middle School
Golden, Colorado

Kathy Glass
San Carlos, California

Alton Greenfield
Minnesota Dept. of Child,
Family & Learning
St. Paul, Minnesota

Sue Hebson
Deerfield High School
Deerfield, Illinois

Carol Jago
Santa Monica High School
Santa Monica, California

Diane Kepner
Oakland, California

Lynne Ludwig
Gregory Middle School
Naperville, Illinois

Joan Markos-Horejs
Fox Valley Writing Project
Oshkosh, Wisconsin

James McDermott
South High Community School
Worcester, Massachusetts

Tim McGee
Worland High School
Worland, Wyoming

Mary Jane Mulholland
Lynn Classical High School
Lynn, Massachusetts

Lisa Myers
Englewood, Colorado

Karen Neilsen
Desert Foothills Middle School
Phoenix, Arizona

Jayne Allen Nichols
El Camino High School
Sacramento, California

Mary Nicolini
Penn Harris High School
Mishawaka, Indiana

Lucretia Pannozzo
John Jay Middle School
Katonah, New York

Robert Pavlick
Marquette University
Milwaukee, Wisconsin

Linda Popp
Gregory Middle School
Naperville, Illinois

Caroline Ratliffe
Fort Bend Instructional School District
Sugar Land, Texas

Guerrino Rich
Akron North High School
Akron, Ohio

Shirley Rosson
Alief Instructional School District
Houston, Texas

Alan Ruter
Glenbrook South High School
Glenview, Illinois

Rene Schillenger
Washington, D.C.

Georgianne Schulte
Oak Park Middle School
Oak Park, Illinois

Carol Schultz
Tinley Park, Illinois

Wendell Schwartz
Adlai E. Stevenson High School
Lincolnshire, Illinois

Lynn Snell
Oak Grove School
Green Oaks, Illinois

Hildi Spritzer
Oakland, California

Bill Stone
Plano Senior High School
Plano, Texas

Barbara Thompson
Hazelwood School
Florissant, Missouri

Elma Torres
Orange Grove Instructional
School District
Orange Grove, Texas

Bill Weber
Libertyville High School
Libertyville, Illinois

Darby Williams
Sacramento, California

Hillary Zunin
Napa High School
Napa, California

Table of Contents

O v e r v i e w

What is a daybook and what is it good for? These are the first questions asked about this series, *Daybooks of Critical Reading and Writing*.

The answer is that a daybook is a keepable, journal-like book that helps improve students' reading and writing. *Daybooks* are a tool to promote daily reading and writing in classrooms. By immersing students in good literature and by asking them to respond creatively to it, the *Daybooks* combine critical reading and creative, personal response to literature.

The literature in each *Daybook* has been chosen to complement the selections commonly found in anthologies and the most commonly taught novels. Most of the literature selections are brief and designed to draw students into them by their brevity and high-interest appeal. In addition, each passage has a literary quality that will be probed in the lesson.

Each lesson focuses on a specific aspect of critical reading—that is, the reading skills used by good readers. These aspects of critical reading are summarized in closing statements positioned at the end of each lesson. To organize this wide-ranging analysis into critical reading, the authors have constructed a framework called the "Angles of Literacy."

This framework organizes the lessons and units in the *Daybook*. The five Angles of Literacy described here are:

- marking or annotating the text
- examining the story connections
- looking at a text from multiple perspectives
- studying the language and craft of a text
- focusing on individual authors

The Angles of Literacy are introduced in the first cluster of the *Daybook* and then explored in greater depth in subsequent clusters.

The *Daybook* concept was developed to help teachers with a number of practical concerns:

1. To introduce daily (or at least weekly) critical reading and writing into classrooms

2. To fit into the new configurations offered by block scheduling

3. To create a literature book students can own, allowing them to mark up the literature and write as they read

4. To make an affordable literature book that students can carry home

How to Use the Daybook

As the *Daybooks* were being developed, more than fifty teachers commented on and reviewed the lesson concept and individual lessons and units. From their comments several main uses for the *Daybooks* emerged.

1. BLOCK SCHEDULING

Daybook activities were designed to accommodate block-scheduled class periods. With longer periods, teachers commented on the need to introduce two to four parts to each "block," one of which would be a *Daybook* lesson. The brief, self-contained lessons fit perfectly at the beginning or end of a block and could be used to complement or build upon another segment of the day.

2. ELECTIVES

With the advent of block scheduling, more electives are being added to the curriculum. Course slots now exist once again for poetry, reading for college, creative writing, and contemporary writers. Teachers found a number of different course slots in which to use the *Daybooks*, mostly because of the strong combination of literature, critical reading, and creative writing.

3. CORE READING LIST

For high schools guided by a list of core readings, the *Daybooks* offered a convenient way to add some daily writing and critical reading instruction to classes. Plus, the emphasis on newer, contemporary writers seemed to these teachers to open up the traditional curriculum with new voices.

4. SUPPLEMENTING AN ANTHOLOGY

For literature teachers using older anthologies, the *Daybook* offers an easy, economical means of updating their literature curriculums. The multitude of newer, contemporary authors and wide range of multicultural authors added nicely to literature classes.

The reviewers of the *Daybooks* proved that no two classrooms are alike. While each was unique in its own way, every teacher found uses for the *Daybook* lessons in the classroom. In the end, the usefulness of the *Daybooks* derived from the blend of elements they offer:

- direct instruction on how to read critically
- regular and explicit practice in marking up and annotating texts
- "writing to learn" activities for each day or week
- great selections from contemporary (and often multicultural) literature
- in-depth instruction in how to read literature and write effectively about it

Organization of the Daybooks

Each *Daybook* has 16 units, or clusters, of five lessons. The 80 lessons afford daily work over a single semester or work two or three times each week for an entire year. A lesson is designed to last approximately 30 minutes, although some lessons will surely extend longer, depending on how energetically students attack the writing activities. But the intent throughout was to create brief, potent lessons that integrate quality literature, critical reading instruction, and writing.

The unifying concept behind these lessons is the Angles of Literacy—the idea that a selection can be approached from at least five directions:

- by annotating and marking up the text
- by analyzing the story connections in the literature
- by examining the text from different perspectives
- by studying the language and craft of the writer
- by focusing closely on all of the aspects of a single writer's work

A lesson typically begins with an introduction and leads quickly into a literary selection. Occasionally the purpose is to direct students' attention to a specific aspect of the selection; but just as often students are asked to read and formulate a response on their own. By looking closely at the selection, students are able to discover what can be learned through careful reading. Students are led to look again at the selection and to respond analytically, reflectively, and creatively to what they have read.

boldface terms in glossary

...ette, in literature, a short, vivid desc... or sketch.

villanelle*, a complex and highly-musical verse form that consists of five tercets rhyming *aba*, with a final quatrain rhyming abaa. The first line is used again as the sixth, twelfth, and ...teenth lines. The third line is used...

unit title

focus on critical reading

lesson title

longer, interpretive response to literature

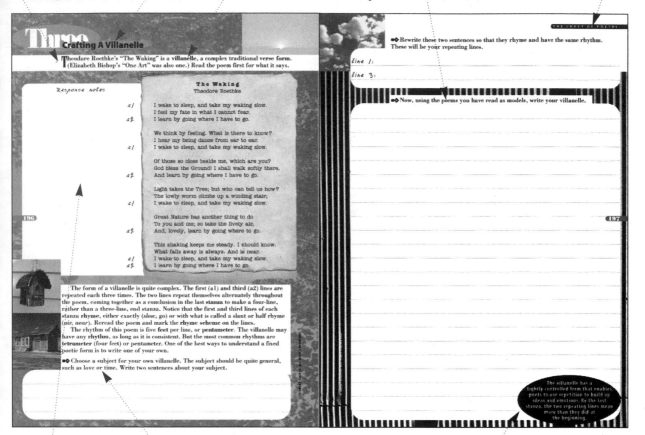

Three
Crafting A Villanelle

Theodore Roethke's "The Waking" is a **villanelle**, a complex traditional verse form. (Elizabeth Bishop's "One Art" was also one.) Read the poem first for what it says.

Response notes

The Waking
Theodore Roethke

a1 I wake to sleep, and take my waking slow.
    I feel my fate in what I cannot fear.
a2 I learn by going where I have to go.

    We think by feeling. What is there to know?
    I hear my being dance from ear to ear.
a1 I wake to sleep, and take my waking slow.

    Of those so close beside me, which are you?
    God bless the Ground! I shall walk softly there,
a2 And learn by going where I have to go.

    Light takes the Tree; but who can tell us how?
    The lowly worm climbs up a winding stair;
a1 I wake to sleep, and take my waking slow.

    Great Nature has another thing to do
    To you and me; so take the lively air,
a2 And, lovely, learn by going where to go.

    This shaking keeps me steady. I should know.
    What falls away is always. And is near.
a1 I wake to sleep, and take my waking slow.
a2 I learn by going where I have to go.

The form of a villanelle is quite complex. The first (a1) and third (a2) lines are repeated each three times. The two lines repeat themselves alternately throughout the poem, coming together as a conclusion in the last **stanza** to make a four-line, rather than a three-line, end stanza. Notice that the first and third lines of each stanza **rhyme**, either exactly (*slow, go*) or with what is called a slant or half rhyme (*air, near*). Reread the poem and mark the **rhyme scheme** on the lines.

The rhythm of this poem is five **feet** per line, or **pentameter**. The villanelle may have any **rhythm**, as long as it is consistent. But the most common rhythms are **tetrameter** (four feet) or pentameter. One of the best ways to understand a fixed poetic form is to write one of your own.

➥ Choose a subject for your own villanelle. The subject should be quite general, such as love or time. Write two sentences about your subject.

➥ Rewrite these two sentences so that they rhyme and have the same rhythm. These will be your repeating lines.

line 1:

line 3:

➥ Now, using the poems you have read as models, write your villanelle.

THE CRAFT OF POETRY

The villanelle has a tightly controlled form that enables poets to use repetition to build up ideas and emotions. By the last stanza, the two repeating lines mean more than they did at the beginning.

space for annotations

initial response activity

summary statement

F r e q u e n t l y   A s k e d   Q u e s t i o n s

One benefit of the extensive field-testing of the *Daybooks* was to highlight right at the beginning several questions about the *Daybooks*.

1. WHAT IS A DAYBOOK ANYWAY?

A daybook used to be "a book in which daily transactions are recorded" or "a diary." Most recently, the word has been used to mean "journal." To emphasize the daily reading and writing, the authors chose the word *daybook* rather than *journal*. And, indeed, the *Daybooks* are much more than journals, in that they include literature selections and instruction in critical reading.

2. ARE STUDENTS SUPPOSED TO WRITE IN THE DAYBOOK?

Yes, definitely. Only by physically marking the text will students become active readers. To interact with a text and take notes as an active reader, students must write in their *Daybooks*. Students will have a written record of their thoughts, questions, brainstorms, annotations, and creative responses. The immediacy of reading and responding on the page is an integral feature of the *Daybooks*. Students will also benefit from the notebook-like aspect, allowing them to double back to earlier work, see progress, store ideas, and record responses. The *Daybook* serves, in a way, like a portfolio. It is one simple form of portfolio assessment.

3. CAN I PHOTOCOPY THESE LESSONS?

No, unfortunately, you cannot. The selections, instruction, and activities are protected by copyright. To copy them infringes on the rights of the authors of the selections and the book. Writers such as Octavio Paz, Toni Morrison, and Ray Bradbury have granted permission for the use of their work in the *Daybook*, and to photocopy their work violates their copyright.

4. CAN I SKIP AROUND IN THE DAYBOOK?

Yes, absolutely. The *Daybooks* were designed to allow teachers maximum flexibility. You can start with some of the later clusters (or units) and then pick up the earlier ones later on in the year. Or you can teach a lesson from here and one from there. But the optimum order of the book is laid out in the table of contents, and students will most likely see the logic and continuity of the book when they start at the beginning and proceed in order.

5. WHAT IS "ANNOTATING A TEXT"? ARE STUDENTS SUPPOSED TO WRITE IN THE MARGIN OF THE BOOK?

Annotating refers to underlining parts of a text, circling words or phrases, highlighting with a colored marker, or taking notes in the margin. Students begin their school years marking up books in kindergarten and end, often in college, writing in the margins of their texts or highlighting key passages. Yet in the years in between—the majority of their school years—students are often forbidden from writing in their books, even though it represents a natural kinesthetic aid for memory and learning.

6. WHY WERE THESE LITERATURE SELECTIONS CHOSEN?

The *Daybooks* are intended to complement high school classrooms, most of which use literature anthologies or have core lists of novels that they teach. In either instance, the literature taught tends to be traditional. Adding contemporary selections is the best way to complement existing curriculums.

The literature was also chosen to illustrate the lesson idea. (A lesson on story characters, for example, needed to present two or three strong characters for study.) So, in addition to being chosen for appeal for students, selections illustrate the specific aspect of critical reading focused on in that lesson.

7. WHAT ARE THE ART AND PHOTOS SUPPOSED TO REPRESENT?

The art program for the *Daybooks* features the work of outstanding contemporary photographers. These photos open each unit and set the tone. Then, within each lesson, a number of smaller, somewhat enigmatic images are used. The purpose behind these images is not to illustrate what is happening in the literature or even to represent an interpretation of it. Rather, the hope is to stretch students' minds, hinting at connections, provoking the imagination, jarring loose a random thought or two about the selection. And, of course, the hope is that students will respond favorably to contemporary expressions of creativity.

8. WHAT ARE THE BOLDFACE TERMS IN THE LESSON ALL ABOUT?

The terms boldfaced in the lessons appear in a glossary in the back of the *Daybook*. The glossary includes key literary terms
   1) that are used in the *Daybook* lessons and
   2) that students are likely to encounter in literature classes.

The glossary is another resource for students to use in reading and reacting to the literature.

Correlation to Writers INC

Like the *Writers INC* handbook, the *Daybooks* will appeal to certain teachers who need versatile, flexible materials and who place a premium on books with high student appeal. Some teachers, by nature, are more eclectic in their teaching approach: others more consistent and patterned. Some teachers place a premium on student interest and relevance more than on structured, predictable lessons. The *Daybooks*, like *Writers INC*, are directed at more eclectic teachers and classrooms.

The *Daybooks* are organized to allow maximum flexibility. You can pick an individual lesson or cluster of lessons in order to feature a certain author or literary selection. Or, you may want to concentrate on a particular area of critical reading. In either case, the *Daybooks*, like *Writers INC*, allow you to pick up the book and use it for days or weeks at a time, then leave it, perhaps to teach a novel or longer writing project, and then return to it again later in the semester. You, not the text, set the classroom agenda.

Another great similarity between the *Daybooks* and the *Writers INC* handbook lies in the approach to writing. Both begin from the premise that writing is, first and foremost, a means of discovery. "Writing to learn" is the common expression for this idea. Only by expression can we discover what lies within us. *Writers INC* introduces this idea in its opening chapter, and the *Daybooks*, by promoting daily writing, give you the tool to make writing a consistent, regular feature of your classes.

But the *Daybooks* only start students on a daily course of reading and writing. Individual writing assignments are initiated but not carried through to final drafts. The purpose of writing in the *Daybooks* is mostly one of discovery, creative expression, clarification of ideas or interpretations, and idea generation. The *Daybooks* are intended to be starting points, places to ruminate and organize thoughts about literature, as opposed to offering definitive instructions about how to craft an essay or write a persuasive letter. That's where *Writers INC* comes in. It picks up where the *Daybooks* leave off, providing everything students need to create a polished essay or literary work.

The accompanying chart correlates writing assignments in the *Daybooks* to *Writers INC*.

Daybook Lesson	**Writing Activity**	**Writers INC reference**
Angles of Literacy		
1. Interacting With a Text	summarize a poem	444, 494, 497
2. Story Connections	create a scenario	331-332, 496
3. Shifting Perspectives	recast a poem	312, 444, 554
4. Language and Craft	complete a word chart	418, 444
5. Focus on the Writer	write dialogue	312, 332, 444

Daybook Lesson	Writing Activity	*Writers INC* reference
Fact Meets Fiction		
1. Historical Details in a Story	evaluate details	111-112, 398, 560-562
2. Objective and Subjective Points of View	examine details	111-112, 398, 428-429
3. Storytelling in Multiple Voices	analyze story structure	410-411, 416
4. Fictionalizing Personal Experience	write a story	105, 286-287, 330
5. Details Tell the Story	analyze a statement	410-411, 560-563
The Nonfiction Novel		
1. Working from Fact	analyze a paragraph	410-411, 415
2. Cinematic Scenes	sketch scenes	311-312
3. Horizontal and Vertical Tellings	classify details	111-112, 339-340, 552
4. Digressions	explain plot structure	339-340, 423
5. Recreating Experience	evaluate nonfiction	131, 339-340, 560-562
Seeing the Landscape		
1. A Landscape of Beauty and Fear	describe a place	66-68, 106, 137, 310
2. Creating a Personal View	personalize a map	478, 555
3. Revealing Character	describe a person	136, 398-400
4. Landscape and Identity	explain an idea	560-563
5. Landscape and Values	write a letter	339-340, 375-376, 403
Perspectives on a Subject: The American Dream		
1. Defining the Dream	analyze a poem	410-411, 414, 444
2. Defining a Subject Through Symbols	create a symbol	425, 555
3. Examining Assumptions	examine a poem	414, 421, 444
4. Satirizing the Subject	write a sonnet	427, 444
5. Reporting an Incident	make inferences	339-340, 560-562

Daybook Lesson	Writing Activity	*Writers INC* reference
Observing and Reflecting		
1. Reflecting on a Small Event	write a poem	311-312, 313, 337-339
2. Philosophical Reflections	extend a poem	330, 337-339, 444
3. Deceptively Simple	write a poem	311-312, 313, 337-339
4. The Poet as Reporter	describe an event	294-297, 554
5. The Poet as Painter	respond to a poem	339, 401, 444
Evaluating Poems		
1. Establishing Criteria	develop criteria	410-411, 414-415
2. Applying the Criteria	analyze a poem	410-411, 414-415
3. Comparing Two Poems	compare two poems	414, 434, 444, 549
4. Sentiment and Sentimentality	judge a poem	356, 414, 444, 560
5. Precise Diction	evaluate a poem's language	356, 410-411, 414, 444
Truman Capote		
1. Local Color	describe a person	106, 136, 421
2. Dualities	analyze characters	410-411, 415
3. Subtle Description	write about fiction	398-400, 402
4. Gothic Style	write a letter	339-340, 375-376
5. Reading Literary Criticism	analyze criticism	131, 339-340, 560
Essentials of Reading		
1. Thinking With the Writer	write a letter	375-376, 554
2. Analyzing Tone	analyze tone	356, 410-411, 425
3. Reading Between the Lines	write to a character	311-312, 398-400
4. Thinking Theme	identify themes	356, 402, 415
5. Author's Purpose	describe author's purpose	120, 545, 560

Daybook Lesson	Writing Activity	*Writers INC* reference
History Through Story		
1. Personal Narratives	write a personal narrative	105, 286-287
2. A Twice-Told Story	revise a personal narrative	8, 105, 286-287, 554
3. Responding Through a Poem	write a poem	286-287, 312-313
4. Vignette as Commentary	draw a scene	311-312, 398-399
5. Fictionalizing History	dramatize a situation	331, 425, 496
Story Structures		
1. As the Story Begins and Ends	analyze a story's beginning	410-411, 415
2. Suspense Through Foreshadowing	analyze foreshadowing	410-411, 415, 421
3. Flashbacks	analyze flashbacks	410-411, 415, 421
4. The Fork in the Road	write a monologue	331-332, 333, 496
5. Unity in the Story	sketch two scenes	311-312, 398-399
Talking Back in Poetry		
1. Historical and Cultural Perspectives	explain a line of a poem	414, 417, 444
2. Understanding Allusions	analyze a poem	410-411, 414, 417, 444
3. Analyzing Allusions	write a paragraph	103-104, 410-411
4. Talking Back with Parody	make a Venn diagram	422, 550
5. Analyzing a Parody	analyze a poem	410-411, 414, 422, 444
Modern Interpretations of Myth		
1. Paying Attention to the Title	answer questions	414, 444
2. Making Connections	evaluate two poems	414, 444, 549
3. Ancient Myths in Modern Dress	interpret a poem	410-411, 414, 444
4. Changing the Tone of a Myth	rewrite a poem	312, 444
5. Changing Perspective	write a monologue	398-400, 419

Angles of Literacy

by Louann Reid

When we view something of potential value, such as a diamond or an antique vase, we often examine it from all sides. We hold it up and slowly turn it, looking first at the front, then the sides and back. Combining information from each perspective, we construct a fuller picture of the object and its worth.

Similarly, we can examine a concept or an idea from several angles, or perspectives, using a variety of approaches to understand a complex concept. Perhaps no concept in education is more complex—or more important—than literacy.

"Literacy" is frequently defined as the ability to read and write. But people also need to be able to read critically, write effectively, draw diagrams, collaborate with others, listen carefully, and understand complex instructions. In short, literacy means being able to do whatever is required to communicate effectively in a variety of situations. Angles of Literacy is the term we use in these *Daybooks* to identify five approaches to becoming literate.

THE FIVE ANGLES

The Angles of Literacy are major perspectives from which to examine a text. Strategies within each angle further define each one. Activities in the *Daybooks* provide students with multiple opportunities to become autonomous users of the strategies on other literature that they will encounter.

The angles are listed in an order that reflects the way that readers and writers first engage with the text. They are encouraged to move gradually from that initial engagement to a more evaluative or critical stance where they study the author's language and craft, life and work. They critique the texts they read and consider what other critics have written. Moving from engagement through interpretation to evaluation is the process that Louise Rosenblatt and later reader-response critics advocate.

In our own work with secondary school students, we have repeatedly seen the value of encouraging students to read and write using all three stages— engagement, interpretation, evaluation. We also know that students sometimes begin at a different stage in the process—perhaps with interpretation rather than engagement. So, our five angles are not meant to be a hierarchy. Students may begin their engagement with the text using any angle and proceed in any order. Depending on the text and the context, readers might start with making personal connections to the stories in an essay. If the text is by an author that the students know well, they might naturally begin by comparing this work to the author's other works.

STRATEGIES

Strategies are plans or approaches to learning. By using some strategies over and over, students can learn to comprehend any text. The *Daybook* activities, such as annotating or visualizing a specific poem, story, or essay, provide students multiple opportunities to develop these strategies. From using this scaffolding students gradually become more independent readers and, ultimately, fully literate.

Because strategies are employed through activities, it may seem at first that they are the same thing. Yet, it is important to remember that a strategy is a purposeful plan. When, as readers, we select a strategy such as underlining key phrases, we have selected this action deliberately to help us differentiate between important information and unimportant information. We may use a double-entry log (an activity) to identify the metaphors in a poem. Our purpose in doing so is to understand figurative language (a strategy). Strategies are purposeful plans, often consisting of one or more activities, to help us comprehend and create.

At the end of each lesson, the strategies are explicitly stated. In a sentence or two, the main point of the activity is noted. When students complete all 80 lessons in a daybook, they will have 80 statements of what they, as active readers, can do to read critically and write effectively.

Reflection is a vital component in helping students understand the use of strategies. After using a particular strategy, students need to step back and consider how the strategy worked or did not. They might think about how an approach or a strategy can change their understanding of what they read and write. Students might ask themselves a series of questions such as: What have I done? What have I learned? What would I do differently next time? How did the angle or strategy affect my understanding? What would I understand differently if I had changed the angle or the strategy?

ACTIVITIES

Each lesson in these *Daybooks* contains activities for students. From rereading to discussing with a partner to making a story chart, students learn how to become better critical readers and more effective writers. Many activities encourage students to write to learn. Other activities encourage students to increase their understanding of a text by visualizing it in a sketch or a graphic organizer. But, as much as possible, the *Daybooks* try to encourage students to make a creative written response with a poem, some dialogue, a character sketch, or some other creative assignment.

We have selected activities that work particularly well with the texts in the lesson and with the strategies we want students to develop. However, as you will see when you and your students use the *Daybooks*, there are several possible activities that could reinforce a particular strategy. You may want to have students try some of these activities, such as making a story chart or using a double-entry log, when they read other texts in class. This would also be another opportunity to have students ask themselves the reflective questions.

Angles of Literacy

ANGLE OF VISION	STRATEGIES	SELECTED ACTIVITIES
Interacting with a Text	• underlining key phrases • writing questions or comments in the margin • noting word patterns and repetitions • circling unknown words • keeping track of the story or idea as it unfolds	• Write down initial impressions. • Re-read. • Write a summary of the poem. • Generate two questions and one "certainty." Then, discuss the questions and statement in a small group.
Making Connections to the Stories within a Text	• paying attention to the stories being told • connecting the stories to one's own experience • speculating on the meaning or significance of incidents	• Make a story chart with three columns—incident in the poem, significance of the incident, related incident in my life. • Write a news story of events behind the story in the poem.

Shifting Perspectives to Examine a Text from Many Points of View	• examining the point of view
	• changing the point of view
	• exploring various versions of an event
	• forming interpretations
	• comparing texts
	• asking "what if" questions
		• Discuss with a partner or small group how you might read a poem differently if:
		    the speaker were female
		    you believe the speaker is a parent
		• Rewrite the text from a different point of view.

Studying the Language and Craft of a Text	• understanding figurative language • looking at the way the author uses words • modeling the style of other writers • studying various kinds of literature	• Use a double-entry log to identify metaphors and the qualities implied by the comparison. • Examine the title of the poem and its relationship to the text.
Focusing on the Writer's Life and Work	• reading what the author says about the writing • reading what others say • making inferences about the connections between an author's life and work • analyzing the writer's style • paying attention to repeated themes and topics in the work by one author	• Read about the poet's life. Then make an inference chart to record evidence from the poet's life, an inference, and a comparison to the poem. • Write an evaluation of the poem. Then read what one or more critics have said about the poem or poet. Finally, write a short response, either agreeing or disagreeing with the critic. Support your ideas with textual evidence.

Responding to Literature Through Writing

by Ruth Vinz

We have found that students' encounters with literature are enriched when they write their way toward understanding. The writing activities in the *Daybooks* are intended to help students explore and organize their ideas and reactions during and after reading. We try to make use of the exploratory and clarifying roles of writing through various activities.

Exploratory assignments include those through which students question, analyze, annotate, connect, compare, personalize, emulate, map, or chart aspects in the literary selections. Generally these assignments aid students' developing interpretations and reactions to the subjects, themes, or literary devices in the literature they are reading. Other writing activities offer students the opportunity to clarify their understanding of what they've read. These assignments lead students to look at other perspectives, determine the significance of what they read, and prioritize, interpret, question, and reflect on initial impressions. Further, students are asked to create literature of their own as a way of applying the concepts they're learning. Writing to clarify also involves students in reflection, where they are asked to think about their reactions and working hypotheses. Taken together, the writing activities represent a series of strategies that students can apply to the complex task of reading literature.

The writing activities included in the *Daybooks* start students on the path toward understanding. We did not take it as the function of the writing activities in this book to lead students through the writing process toward final, finished drafts. Although examples of extensions are included here in the Teacher's Guide, the writing in the *Daybooks* introduces first draft assignments that may lead into more formal writing if you, as the teacher, so choose.

You will have your own ideas about assisting students with the writing activities or extending the writing beyond the *Daybooks*. We think it's important for you to remind students that the writing in which they engage is useful for their reading outside the *Daybooks*. For example, students may use various types of maps, charts, or diagrams introduced in the *Daybooks* when they read a novel. They may find that the response notes become a strategy they use regularly. Once exposed to imitation and modeling, students may find these useful tools for understanding an author's style, language, or structure. If your students develop a conscious awareness of the strategies behind the particular writing activities, they can apply these in other reading situations.

Writing assignments to explore and to clarify students' developing interpretations are incorporated in two types of activities, both of which are elaborated on below.

WRITING ABOUT LITERATURE

You will find activities in every cluster of lessons that call upon students to write about the literature they are reading. We developed these writing assignments to help facilitate, stimulate, support, and shape students' encounters with literature. We think the assignments have four purposes:

(1) to connect the literature to the students' personal experiences; (2) to re-examine the text for various purposes (language and craft, connections with other texts, shifting perspectives, developing interpretations); (3) to develop hypotheses, judgments, and critical interpretations; (4) to apply the idea behind the lesson to a new literary text or situation.

The types of writing we have used to fulfill these purposes are:

1. Response Notes

Students keep track of their initial responses to the literature by questioning, annotating, and marking up the text in various ways. The response notes are used to get students in the habit of recording what they are thinking while reading. Seldom do we begin by telling them what and how to write in this space. Many times we circle back and ask them to build on what they have written with a particular focus or way of responding. In the response notes, students are encouraged to make personal connections, re-examine text, jot down ideas for their own writing, and monitor their changing responses.

2. Personal Narrative

Students write personal stories that connect or relate to what they have read. In some cases, the narratives tell the stories of students' prior reading experiences or how a literary selection relates to their life experiences. Other activities use personal narrative to apply and refine students' understanding of narrative principles.

3. Idea Fund

Students collect ideas for writing—catalogs, lists, charts, clusters, diagrams, double-entry logs, sketches, or maps. These forms of idea gathering are useful for analyzing particular literary selections and will aid the initial preparation for longer pieces of critical analysis.

4. Short Response

Students write summaries; paraphrase main themes or ideas; and compose paragraphs of description, exposition, explanation, evaluation, and interpretation.

5. Analysis

Students write short analyses that take them beyond summarizing the literary selection or their personal reactions to it. The analytic activities engage students in recognizing symbols and figures of speech and the links between events, characters, or images. Again, these short analytical responses are intended to prepare students for longer, critical interpretation that you, as a teacher, might assign.

6. Speculation

Students' speculations are encouraged by writing activities that engage them in predicting, inferring, and imagining. "What if…," "How might…," and "Imagine that…" are all ways in which students are invited to see further possibilities in the literature they read.

Students use writing to record and reflect on their reactions and interpretations. At times, students are asked to share their writing with others. Such sharing is another form of reflection through which students have an opportunity to "see again" their own work in the context of what others have produced.

The writing activities in the *Daybooks* will help students connect what they read with what they experience and with what they write, and also to make connections between the literary selections and literary techniques. The activities encourage students to experiment with a range of forms, choose a range of focuses, and reflect on what they have learned from these. We hope the writing serves to give students access to a kind of literary experience they can value and apply in their future reading.

WRITING LITERATURE

Within a literary work, readers find a writer's vision, but readers also co-create the vision along with the writer and learn from his or her craft. We've asked our students to write literature of their own as a way of responding to what they read. Through writing literature, students can explore facets of the original work or use the techniques of a variety of authors. Here are a number of the activities introduced in the *Daybooks*:

1. Take the role of writer

Students write imaginative reconstructions of gaps in a text by adding another episode, adding dialogue, rewriting the ending, adding a section before or after the original text, adding characters, changing the setting, or creating dream sequences. Such imaginative entries into the text require that students apply their knowledge of the original.

2. Imitation and Modeling

The idea of modeling and imitation is not new. Writers learn from other writers. The modeling activities are intended to help students "read like a writer." In these activities, students experiment with nuances of expression, syntactic and other structural principles, and apply their knowledge of literary devices (for example, *rhythm, imagery, metaphor*). One goal in educating students with literature is to make explicit what writers do. One way to achieve the goal is to provide models that illustrate various principles of construction.

3. Original Pieces

Students write poems, character sketches, monologues, dialogues, episodes, vignettes, and descriptions as a way to apply the knowledge about language and craft they are gaining through their reading.

4. Living Others' Perspectives

Writing from others' points of view encourages students to step beyond self to imagine other perspectives. Students write from a character's point of view, compose diary entries or letters, explain others' positions or opinions, and other reactions to a situation. These writing activities encourage students to explore the concerns of others and to project other perspectives through their writing.

The writing becomes a record of students' developing and changing ideas about literature. By the time students have finished all of the writing in this book, they will have used writing strategies that can assist them in all future reading.

Reading, Writing, and Assessment

by Fran Claggett

As teachers, we all cope with the complexities of assessing student performance. We must be careful readers of student work, attentive observers of student participation in various activities, and focused writers in responding to student work. We must understand the value of rewarding what students do well and encouraging them to improve. Above all, we need to make the criteria for assessment clear to students.

THE DAYBOOKS

The *Daybooks* provide visible accounts of many aspects of the reading process. Students record all the various permutations of active reading and writing. In the current view of most teachers and researchers, reading is a process of constructing meaning through transactions with a text. In this view, the individual reader assumes responsibility for interpreting a text guided not only by the language of the text but also by the associations, cultural experiences, and prior knowledge that the reader brings to the interpretive task. Meaning does not reside solely within the words on the page. Our view of reading emphasizes the role of the reader. Construction of meaning, rather than the gaining and displaying of knowledge should be the goal of reading instruction. This rule is reflected throughout the *Daybooks*, which guide students in how to read, respond to, interpret, and reflect on carefully selected works of literature.

Within these lessons, students interact with a text from five angles of literacy. The *Daybooks* make it possible for both students and teachers to track students' increasing sophistication in using the angles to make sense of their reading. Through the strategies presented in the lessons, students learn to express their understanding of a text. They will do such things as show their understanding of figurative language and the importance of form; write about how characters are developed and change; and demonstrate their understanding of how a piece of literature develops.

THE ROLE OF THE TEACHER

The teacher is critical to the *Daybook* agenda. Conceivably, a teacher could pass out the *Daybooks* and turn the students loose, but that would not result in the carefully guided reading and writing that is intended. Rather, the teachers are central to student success. Because of the format of the *Daybooks*, lessons are short, each taking no more than a normal class period. They are intended to be complete in themselves, yet most teachers will see that there are numerous opportunities for extensions, elaborations, further readings, group work, and writing. The Teacher's Guide provides some suggestions; you will think of many others. The *Daybooks* offer guidelines for reading and thinking, for writing and drawing used in the service of reading. They also provide many opportunities for students to write pieces of their own, modeling, responding, interpreting, and reflecting on the pieces that they have read. Many of these pieces might lead to later revision, refining, group response, and editing. It is the teacher, however, who knows the students well enough to see which pieces would be worthwhile to work with and which it is best to leave as exercises rather than completed works.

In assessing the *Daybooks*, it is important to remember to look at the students' growing facility with the processes of reading. As is true with all learning, there will be false starts, abandoned practices, and frustrations, yet also illuminations, progress, and occasional epiphanies. No music teacher ever graded every attempt at mastering a piece of music. We, too, must resist the urge—honed by years of assessing only products or finished papers—of overassessing the *Daybooks*. We must consider them the place where students are free to think things through, change their minds, even start over. But you can be alert to what the student is doing well, what is frustrating, what needs more time. To that end, we have provided a chart which may be useful in getting a sense of how students are progressing in using angles of literacy. By duplicating the chart for each student, you can track progress through the lessons. We would like to encourage the idea of jotting down notations as you work with students during the class period or look over the *Daybooks* after class. In this way, you can amass a sizable amount of information over a grading period. Coupled with a student self-assessment such as the one included here, you will have tangible evidence of achievement in the *Daybooks*.

STUDENT SELF-ASSESSMENT

A student self-assessment chart is a useful adjunct to the teacher chart. This particular format works well as it asks students to consider interest, value, and participation as well as quality.

Followed by the self-assessment essay, it provides valuable insight into the student's sense of accomplishment.

INDIVIDUAL STUDENT EIGHT-WEEK ASSESSMENT CHART

The columns for each week's lessons can be used in different ways. We suggest the number system: a 5 for insightful, imaginative thinking or responding, a 1 for a minimal attempt. Some teachers prefer the check, check-plus, check-minus system. There is even room, if you turn the chart sideways, to make some notations.

Angles of Literacy

INTERACTING WITH A TEXT	I	II	III	IV	V	VI	VII	VIII
The student demonstrates understanding by using interactive strategies such as:								
underlining key phrases								
writing questions or comments in the margin								
noting word patterns and repetitions								
circling unknown words								
keeping track of ideas as they unfold								

MAKING CONNECTIONS	I	II	III	IV	V	VI	VII	VIII
The student makes connections to the stories with a text by:								
paying attention to the stories in the text								
connecting ideas and themes in the text to personal ideas, experience, feelings, and knowledge								
making connections to other texts, movies, television shows, or other media								

SHIFTING PERSPECTIVES	I	II	III	IV	V	VI	VII	VIII
The student is able to shift perspectives to examine a text from many points of view. When prompted, the student will engage in such strategies as these:								
examining the point of view								
changing the point of view								
exploring various versions of an event, forming interpretations								
comparing texts and responding to "what if" questions to deepen understanding								

STUDYING THE LANGUAGE AND CRAFT OF A TEXT	I	II	III	IV	V	VI	VII	VIII
The student will demonstrate an understanding of the way language and craft operate in a text. Specifically, the student will:								
show how imagery, metaphor, and figurative language are central to literature								
demonstrate an understanding of how an author's vocabulary and use of language are integral to the overall work								
use modeling to demonstrate an understanding of style and form								
demonstrate understanding of various genres and forms of literature								

FOCUSING ON THE WRITER	I	II	III	IV	V	VI	VII	VIII
The student will demonstrate a rich understanding of a single writer's work, including:								
interpreting short texts by the author								
making inferences about the connections between an author's life and work								
analyzing the writer's style								
drawing conclusions about repeated themes and topics in an author's work								
evaluating a text or comparing works by the same author								

END OF TERM STUDENT SELF-ASSESSMENT CHART

Fill out the chart by naming or describing the work you have completed in the *Daybooks*. Since the *Daybooks* are focused on the reading of and writing about literature, it might be useful to list the actual texts you have read. To measure your achievement, think about the work you did as you explored the angles of vision for each text.

For each item, use the numbers 1 (low) to 5 (high) to indicate the four aspects of your involvement. Following completion of the chart, write the Self-Assessment Essay.

WORKS OF LITERATURE READ	LEVEL OF INTEREST	LEVEL OF VALUE	DEGREE OF PARTICIPATION	QUALITY OF PARTICIPATION

STUDENT SELF-ASSESSMENT ESSAY

After you have filled out this chart, write a self-evaluation essay, reflecting on your work in the *Daybooks* for the past term and articulating ideas about what you hope to achieve in the next. Refer specifically to the texts listed in the chart, elaborating on your assessment of a text's interest or value, commenting on reasons for the degree of your involvement, or explaining why you have assessed the quality of your work as you have.

M o d e l i n g :   A n   O v e r v i e w

by Fran Claggett

The overriding goal in modeling is to help students become discerning readers and inventive, perceptive writers. Modeling works well with students of all ability levels, whether homogeneously or heterogeneously grouped. It is especially effective in working with second-language students. My own classroom experience, as well as testimony from writers and researchers, indicates that modeling closely resembles the natural stages we go through in the acquisition of language. Many writers have talked about how, during their formative years, they either consciously or unconsciously imitated the styles of other writers whom they admired. Here, I will focus on the metacognitive aspects of modeling, making the processes of thinking and learning explicit for students, urging them to explore their own ways of making sense not only of what they read but what they write.

USING MODELING IN THE CLASSROOM

Through various modeling experiences, students learn the relationships among form, structure, and style. They learn to slow down their reading in order to appreciate the ways authors create specific effects. A critical aspect of using modeling with all students is the selection of the work to be modeled. The teacher must be clear on the focus of the assignment, allow for the margin of success by selecting works for modeling that are within the students' grasp, and make certain that students enter into the metacognitive aspect of the exercise.

Some of the ways that modeling can be integrated into classroom assignments:

1. As a catalyst for writing, particularly for reluctant writers. It immediately provides a structure and takes away much of the threat of the blank page.

2. As an introduction to poetry. Again, much of the onus is gone when students first model a poem, then discover the form by analyzing their own work as well as the original.

3. To encourage close reading of a text. As part of the study of a novel—particularly a difficult one stylistically—have students choose a representative passage (they decide what is representative), model it, then do a structural analysis of it. This exercise enhances both their understanding of the content of the original (it slows down their reading) and their grasp of the author's style. Students often work together in pairs or groups on this activity.

4. To teach awareness of diction. Choose a passage and, as a class, analyze its tone by exploring the use of diction, detail, and syntax. They might even write an analysis of the passage. Either after or before the analysis, students choose a different subject from that of the original and emulate the passage, working consciously to create a particular tone or effect. Students can also write emulations of each other's work, accompanied by an analysis and critique.

5. As a way of teaching English language sentence patterns to second-language learners. By modeling, students are able to internalize the natural flow of English sentences.

6. As part of an intensive author study. Students read a variety of works (short stories, essays, poems, novels, plays) by a single author. They select sections they believe to be representative of the author's style and analyze them from the standpoint of diction, tone, and main idea. They should model a short section. Their final piece in this assignment, which also involves secondary source biographical research, is to write a full imitation of the style of this author, showing through their choice of subject matter, genre, syntax, voice, and tone that they have developed and internalized a familiarity with the author's style.

KINDS OF MODELING TAUGHT IN THE DAYBOOKS

Emulation	replace word for word by function
Spinoff Modeling	respond to original content; retain tone, perhaps first line
Fixed Form Modeling	follow the pattern or form of the original (e.g., a sonnet)
Structural Modeling	model the thought progressions of the original
The Paralog	create a parallel dialogue with the author
Style Modeling	write a substantial piece in the style of an author

ANGLES OF LITERACY

Unit Overview

"Angles of Literacy" encourages students to develop the strategies of active reading: interacting with the text, making connections to what they read, shifting perspectives, analyzing the author's craft, and examining an author's life. As they explore the poetry of Anne Sexton, students will practice these techniques and, as a result, become more perceptive readers.

Literature Focus

	Lesson	Literature
1.	Interacting With a Text	**Anne Sexton,** "To a Friend Whose Work Has Come to Triumph" (Poetry)
		Anne Sexton, "The Starry Night" (Poetry)
2.	Story Connections	
3.	Shifting Perspectives	
4.	Language and Craft	
5.	Focus on the Writer	**Maxine Kumin,** from "A Friendship Remembered" (Nonfiction)
		Anne Sexton, "The Fury of Overshoes" (Poetry)

Reading Focus

1. Active readers engage in a dialogue with the author as they read. They interact with the work of literature by underlining, asking questions, drawing, and jotting down ideas.

2. Active readers look not only for the stories behind a work—such as myths or biographical information—but also for experiences in their own lives that parallel the stories in the work.

3. Shifting perspectives in a text will help you develop insight into the original work as well as possibilities for your own writing.

4. Looking closely at language and form increases your ability to read sympathetically, almost as if you were reading as the writer would.

5. Reading multiple works by an author and learning about his or her life extends your understanding of the author's work.

Writing Focus

1. Summarize your understanding of a poem.
2. Write about a personal experience.
3. Recast a poem into another form.
4. Comment on a poem's language.
5. Write a dialogue in which you and Anne Sexton discuss one of her poems.

One Interacting With a Text

Critical Reading

FOCUS

FOCUS

Active readers make an effort to interact with what they read.

BACKGROUND

Anne Sexton is one of the most widely read poets of recent decades. Dying by her own hand at age forty-five in 1974, she left behind an extraordinary body of work. Her poems have often been categorized as confessional because they reveal intensely personal and painful perceptions and feelings.

➤ Sexton grew up in a conventional middle-class Massachusetts family, married while in her teens, and worked for a while as a fashion model. After the birth of her second daughter, Sexton suffered a severe breakdown. Her therapist suggested that she try writing poetry to combat the illness. Sexton joined a Boston writing group that included such poets as Robert Lowell, Maxine Kumin, George Starbuck, and Sylvia Plath. The next eighteen years of creative work resulted in twelve books of published poetry and a Pulitzer Prize for *Live or Die*. Anne Sexton said that "When I'm writing, I know I'm doing the thing I was born to do."

FOR DISCUSSION AND REFLECTION

➤ As students examine how one reader has annotated the poem "To a Friend Whose Work Has Come to Triumph," ask them to comment on what this reader has marked in the poem. (Responses will vary.)

➤ What kind of words and phrases are circled? (Readers often mark images that they find intriguing but puzzling.)

➤ What did the reader note in the margins? (Active readers often comment on observations that they make as they read. They record their own process of coming to understand the poem.)

➤ What does the reader's comment that begins "I still don't completely understand" suggest to you about this person's attitude towards reading poetry? (One answer is that understanding and comprehension are something that you come to over time rather than simply get at a first reading. This reader will most likely go back and read the poem again.)

Writing

QUICK ASSESS

Do students' summaries:

✓ demonstrate understanding of the poem?

✓ draw on ideas from their annotations and drawings?

After annotating "The Starry Night" for themselves, students are asked to write a brief summary of the poem. In order to help them get started, ask students to think about the character "I" in this poem. What kind of person does he or she seem to be? What is he or she doing? How is he or she feeling?

READING AND WRITING EXTENSIONS

➤ Show students a reproduction of Vincent van Gogh's painting. Have them write a story set within the world of this image.

➤ Don McLean wrote a song called "Vincent"; it begins "Starry, starry night. / Paint your palette blue and grey, / Look out on a summer's day, / With eyes that know the darkness in my soul." Play the song for students and ask them to compare it with Sexton's poem.

Two Story Connections

Critical Reading

FOCUS

Active readers should try to connect to a text by relating their experience to the story being told.

BACKGROUND

Daedalus was a master builder imprisoned with his son Icarus on the island of Crete. Longing for home, Daedalus searched for a means of escape. What he found were feathers from seabirds, and with these he fashioned wings for himself and Icarus. As they prepared to fly, Daedalus warned his son to follow a course midway between earth and heaven, in case the sun should scorch his feathers if he flew too high, or the water makes them heavy if he flew too low. Drawn on by his eagerness for the open sky, Icarcus left his guide and soared upwards until he came too close to the blazing sun; it melted the wax binding his feathers. With his wings ruined, Icarus plunged into the sea and died.

➤ Sexton's title is a reference to W. B. Yeats's poem "To a Friend Whose Work Has Come to Nothing."

FOR DISCUSSION AND REFLECTION

➤ How is Daedalus's warning to his son Icarus similar to warnings parents give their children? (Parents want to keep their children safe and are always urging them not to take chances, not to fly too high or too low.)

➤ Why do these warnings often fall on deaf ears? (Teenagers want to test their own limits and to explore the world around them for themselves. Most don't want to follow in their parents' wake.)

➤ Why do you think Anne Sexton uses this ancient story of Daedalus as a framework for "To a Friend Whose Work Has Come to Triumph? (Sexton is comparing her friend with the intrepid Icarus and suggesting that an artist lives for a moment spent in the "hot eye" of the sun. Sexton congratulates her friend for having achieved this moment.)

Writing

QUICK ASSESS

Do students' responses:

✓ describe the setting and action?

✓ explore their reflections on the experience?

Students are asked to imagine a scenario that might have inspired "The Starry Night." They are then instructed to write about a time when some aspect of nature made them reflect on their life. Begin by brainstorming times when such reflective moments most often occur: watching a sunset, hiking in the mountains, sitting on a chairlift, during long car rides, staring into a bank of clouds, near bodies of water. Encourage students to include concrete details about the setting as they write.

READING AND WRITING EXTENSIONS

➤ Assign students the task of finding a safe outdoor spot where they can sit undisturbed for twenty minutes and record everything they see, hear, smell, taste, and feel during that time. These observations can later be turned into a poem in which they reflect on the interior as well as the exterior landscape.

➤ Bring in a collection of landscape paintings and have students write an interior monologue of an imaginary person who is walking through the scene of one of the paintings or sitting just outside the picture frame.

Three Shifting Perspectives

Critical Reading

FOCUS

Asking "what if" questions will help a reader uncover the underlying meaning of a text.

BACKGROUND

The story of Icarus has inspired many artists, including the painter Pieter Brueghel and poets W. H. Auden, William Carlos Williams, and Anne Sexton. These artists expect their audiences to be familiar with the legend of Icarus and to be comfortable with the idea that they are using this story for their own purposes. In "To a Friend Whose Work Has Come to Triumph," Anne Sexton, herself a poet aspiring to soar, congratulates W. D. Snodgrass for winning the Pulitzer Prize in 1960 for *Heart's Needle*.

➤ In her own work, as well as in her personal life, Sexton often shocked. She liked to arrive about ten minutes late for her own performances. She would saunter to the podium, light a cigarette, kick off her shoes, and in a throaty voice say, "I'm going to read a poem that tells you what kind of a poet I am, what kind of a woman I am, so if you don't like it you can leave." Like Icarus, Sexton was drawn to the sun.

FOR DISCUSSION AND REFLECTION

➤ Students are asked to speculate with a partner about how their reading of Anne Sexton's poem "To a Friend Whose Work Has Come to Triumph" would change if certain aspects of the text were changed. Have volunteers share with the class what they talked about with their partners. Chart their insights so that students can identify the common ways writers shift perspectives.

➤ What does Sexton choose to use from the original story? (Student responses might include Icarus's bold approach to the sun, his willingness to ignore the warnings of authority to play it safe.)

➤ What does Sexton choose to discard? (She never mentions the father's concern for his child or any suggestion that Icarus might have felt fear at setting out with his wings.)

Writing

QUICK ASSESS

Do students' new versions:

✓ demonstrate an understanding of the Icarus myth?

✓ reflect an understanding of how shifting perspectives alters a story?

In order to recast the story of Icarus for their own purposes, students should first determine what it is about the myth that intrigues them. Once they have determined this, invite students to explore a variety of forms for their own retelling.

READING AND WRITING EXTENSIONS

➤ Show students a reproduction of Pieter Brueghel's "Icarus" and then have students read W. H. Auden's "Museé des Beaux Arts," William Carlos Williams's "Landscape with the Fall of Icarus," and Michael Hamburger's "Lines on Brueghel's Icarus."

➤ Have students read poems from Sexton's collection *Transformations*, retellings of common fairytales.

Four Language and Craft

Critical Reading

FOCUS

In *Poetic Meter and Poetic Form*, Paul Fussell writes that "The poet who understands the sonnet form is the one who has developed an instinct for exploiting the principal of imbalance."

BACKGROUND

Anne Sexton wrote her poem "To a Friend Whose Work Has Come to Triumph" in the form of a Shakespearean sonnet. This is a fixed verse form of Italian origin consisting of fourteen lines that are five-foot iambics rhyming according to a prescribed scheme in which a problem is introduced and a solution offered. In a Shakespearean sonnet, the solution is often a paradox or quick bit of wit. The solution Sexton offers is her own answer to the question in line 12, "Who cares that he fell back to the sea?" For her, Icarus's death is preferable to Daedalus's life: "See him acclaiming the sun and come plunging down / while his sensible daddy goes straight into town." Like Shakespeare, Sexton has ended her poem with mock-logic.

FOR DISCUSSION AND REFLECTION

➤ Why might Anne Sexton have chosen to write this poem as a Shakespearean sonnet? Why would anyone choose such a challenging form to work within? (Student answers might include that the form provides a structure for the poet's complex ideas, that the form reminds readers of other poems they have read, that it is a way for a poet to demonstrate her skill.)

➤ What do the final lines of "To a Friend Whose Work Has Come to Triumph" say to you about Sexton's attitude towards Icarus's dangerous flight path compared with the safer journey of his father? (Sexton applauds Icarus's achievement and compares it with her friend's "triumph." She considers Daedalus's flight obviously sensible but one unworthy of praise.)

➤ Ask students to read the poem out loud and identify Sexton's rhyme scheme. What is the effect of the rhymes on a reader? (The rhyming pattern holds the poem together, and the final couplet's rhyme reinforces the poet's mockery of Daedalus.)

Writing

QUICK ASSESS

Do students' charts:

✓ identify words and phrases from the poem that intrigue them?

✓ include reasons for choosing these lines?

Students are asked to reread "The Starry Night" and to identify words and phrases that they found interesting or provocative. They are then invited to comment on why these lines struck them. Model this process for students with a line or two from the poem that struck you. Copying your reasons for choosing a phrase at the top of their chart can help students who are unsure of how to begin.

READING AND WRITING EXTENSIONS

➤ Read together Shakespeare's Sonnet 116, "Let me not to the marriage of true minds," in which Shakespeare defines love as steadfast, unshakable, focused, and unchangeable until the final couplet. Have students compare this poem with Sexton's sonnet.

➤ Ask students to write about whether they prefer the short, passionate life of Icarus or the less exciting, but longer life of Daedalus.

Five Focus on the Writer

Critical Reading

FOCUS

In her inscription of Maxine Kumin's copy of *To Bedlam and Part Way Back*, Sexton wrote, "For Max, who encouraged me with all of these poems, and 'halfway' wrote some, and who is all the way my friend, my friend."

BACKGROUND

In her biography of Anne Sexton, Diane Wood Middlebrook explained that "Anne Sexton began writing poetry as a teenager, like many of us, then stopped, like most of us. She began writing again when she was a suicidal woman undergoing psychiatric treatment, with two young children of her own. Sexton spent a good deal of her adult life pursuing associations that lead back into childhood. She was drawn again and again to painful feelings towards her family. It became clear to her that the past exists only in versions, which differed according to our motives at the moment of recall."

➤ In "A Friendship Remembered," the poet Maxine Kumin describes her relationship with the bewitching and exasperating Anne Sexton. She describes how they would talk on the phone for hours, long past when reason and responsibility dictated that their conversations should end.

FOR DISCUSSION AND REFLECTION

➤ Have you ever had a friend with whom you loved talking into the night? What kinds of things did you talk about? Have students discuss what it was about this person that made him or her the perfect phone companion.

➤ Based upon this excerpt from Maxine Kumin's essay, what do you speculate kept these two friends talking? (Responses will vary.)

➤ How does sharing something you are writing with a friend you trust help you write? (Encourage students to consider how they are often very critical of their own work and how the encouragement of a friend can help them to see what is good in what they have written. Revision can come later. First a writer needs to get something down on the page. Kumin and Sexton helped each other with this initial stage of creation.)

Writing

QUICK ASSESS

Do students' dialogues:

✓ find ways to comment on Sexton's poem that are critical yet supportive?

✓ refer to specifics from the poem?

Students are asked to write an imaginary conversation between themselves and Anne Sexton about her poem "The Fury of Overshoes." Before they begin, have students share their first impressions of the poem with a partner.

READING AND WRITING EXTENSIONS

➤ Read to the class Maxine Kumin's poem "For Anne at Passover," from her collection *Halfway*. Ask students to discuss what this poem reveals about Kumin and Sexton's friendship.

➤ Have students write about what they remember of being so small that "you couldn't / buckle your own / overshoe / or tie your own / shoe / or cut your own meat . . . ."

Unit Overview

In this unit, students explore how and why writers use historical experiences and details. Through reading a variety of excerpts from both fiction and nonfiction, they will learn about using multiple narrators, fictionalizing personal experiences, and blending objective and subjective points of view and begin to appreciate how writers achieve powerful and dramatic effects through the use of these techniques.

Literature Focus

	Lesson	Literature
1.	Historical Details in a Story	**Charles Johnson,** from *Middle Passage* (Novel)
2.	Objective and Subjective Points of View	**N. Scott Momaday,** from *The Way to Rainy Mountain* (Nonfiction)
3.	Storytelling in Multiple Voices	**N. Scott Momaday,** from *The Way to Rainy Mountain* (Nonfiction)
4.	Fictionalizing Personal Experience	**Julia Alvarez,** from "Snow" from *How the García Girls Lost Their Accents* (Novel)
5.	Details Tell the Story	**Tim O'Brien,** "How to Tell a True War Story," from *The Things They Carried* (Nonfiction)

Reading Focus

1. Writers use historical details and situations in their fictional works to give an air of believability, to heighten the reality of a situation, and to create a sense of drama.
2. An objective point of view provides readers with factual information. The subjective point of view gives information about how events have been interpreted by the author, narrator, or characters.
3. Writers sometimes use multiple narrators to try to present some of the perspectives on a story. Readers need to identify who is telling the story and what each contributes to the larger idea.
4. Writers often fictionalize their experiences to enhance the dramatic effect.
5. The details of a story can sometimes be far more important to the reader than any abstractions or generalizations that are made.

Writing Focus

1. Examine an author's use of historical detail.
2. Complete a chart about objective and subjective details.
3. Answer questions about multiple accounts of a story.
4. Write a fictionalized account of a personal experience.
5. Explain and respond to an author's statement.

One Historical Details in a Story

Critical Reading

FOCUS

In *Middle Passage* the narrator Rutherford declares, "As I live, they so shamed me I wanted their ageless culture to be my own ...."

BACKGROUND

Charles Johnson (born 1948) won the National Book Award in 1990 for his novel *Middle Passage*, the story of an educated slave who ends up a stowaway on the ironically named *Republic*. The novel details Rutherford's experiences on the slave ship with 40 members of the Allmuseri tribe who have been captured and are to be sold as slaves. Johnson's novel looks at Rutherford alongside the Allmuseri, and both of them in contrast to Westerners who perpetuate the institution of slavery.

➤ Charles Johnson has argued in his critical study *Being and Race* (1988) that African American authors have been too narrow in their description of African American life in this country and that they have repeated the limited observations of sociologists and historians. As a result, many African American writers have participated in their own stereotyping. Johnson's writing is dedicated to breaking those stereotypes. *Middle Passage* tells the story of an educated, recently emancipated slave from Indiana who ends up in New Orleans and who, as a result of his attempt to escape marriage, ends up as a stowaway on the ironically named slave ship *The Republic*. Rutherford is a rogue and a trickster. His experiences with the members of the Allmuseri, who rebel on the ship, change Rutherford forever.

FOR DISCUSSION AND REFLECTION

➤ Why is Rutherford drawn to the Allmuseri? (They possess qualities of character that he admires: hard-working, non-violent, honest.)

➤ What is unusual about Charles Johnson's choice of Rutherford as a narrator for a story about a slave ship? (Rutherford, himself a black man, is part of the crew, rather than part of the cargo.)

➤ Does the fact that Rutherford is black make him more or less reliable as a narrator? (Student answers will vary but may suggest that Rutherford seems to sympathize with the captives and, therefore, possibly sees their plight more clearly.)

Writing

QUICK ASSESS

Do students' explanations:

✓ identify historical detail?

✓ include their judgment of Johnson's effectiveness?

✓ show how details lend believability to the episode?

Students are asked to explain how Johnson makes use of detail to create drama. Have them reread the passage and underline information about conditions on the ship and conditions of the slave trade that Johnson has conveyed to readers.

READING AND WRITING EXTENSIONS

➤ Invite students to find an American history or social studies textbook and turn to the section on the slave trade. Read a passage from the text aloud and then ask them to compare the impact of this kind of telling with Charles Johnson's account.

➤ Have students write an interior monologue for the Allmuseri mother. What is going through her mind on the ship when she approaches Rutherford? What are her fears? What does she hope for?

Two Objective and Subjective Points of View

Critical Reading

FOCUS

N. Scott Momaday has written: "...the way to Rainy Mountain is preeminently the history of an idea, man's idea of himself ...."

BACKGROUND

N. Scott Momaday is a Native American who has written widely about his Kiowa heritage. Momaday grew up on an Oklahoma farm and on Southwestern reservations. His first novel, *House Made of Dawn*, is narrated from several different points of view and presents the dilemma of a young man returning home to his Kiowa pueblo after serving in the U.S. Army. The book won the 1969 Pulitzer Prize for fiction. *The Way to Rainy Mountain* retells the history of the Kiowa people through a mixture of objective detail and subjective narration.

➤ Momaday has said that "From the time I could first function in language, I have been in love with words. How I gloried to hear my father tell the old Kiowa stories, which existed only at the level of the human voice. And how I loved my mother to invent stories in which I played the principal part. In my earliest years I lived in a home that was informed by the imagination, by the telling of stories and the celebration of language."

FOR DISCUSSION AND REFLECTION

➤ What does Momaday refer to when he writes of the northern Plains? (Point to this area on a map.)

➤ What is the significance of the destruction of the buffalo described in Momaday's story? (Buffalo once roamed the Plains in huge numbers, but "the wild herds were destroyed." The Kiowa people, too, are endangered.)

➤ What do you think Momaday means when he says that "The verbal tradition . . . has suffered a deterioration in time"? (Answers will vary. Help students to think about how writing has supplanted storytelling as a vehicle for preserving history.)

➤ How would you describe the genre Momaday employs? (*The Way to Rainy Mountain* is both an objective account of his people and a subjective retelling of the stories Momaday knows.)

Writing

QUICK ASSESS

Do students' charts:

✔ distinguish between objective and subjective details?

✔ include several examples of each kind?

✔ follow the sequence of events Momaday describes?

Students are asked to list objective and subjective details describing the Kiowa people's journey. Before they begin, check that every student clearly understands the difference between the two.

READING AND WRITING EXTENSIONS

➤ Read Momaday's poem "Rainy Mountain Cemetery" from *In the Presence of the Sun* (1992) and ask students once again to list the objective and subjective details they can find.

➤ In order to explore the poetics of Momaday's prose, have students choose lines and phrases from this excerpt and arrange them into a found poem called "The Way to Rainy Mountain."

Three Storytelling in Multiple Voices

Critical Reading

FOCUS

Momaday on his writing:

"With every attempt to write a line I have learned something. I have tried to keep my mind alive for the sake of learning. That is my reason for doing what I do and for being who I am."

BACKGROUND

N. Scott Momaday explains that "I have been called 'the man made of words.' It is an identity that pleases me. Reading and writing, talking, telling stories, listening, remembering, and thinking have been the cornerstones of my existence." Momaday calls upon his Kiowa background to give us echoes of an ancient oral tradition. *The Way to Rainy Mountain* does not read like a typical historical novel, proceeding from one event in sequential order to the next. Instead, Momaday offers readers a collection of voices, artistically arranged, telling the story from various points of view.

FOR DISCUSSION AND REFLECTION

➤ What clues can you find in the first paragraph of the excerpt to identify the narrator? (This is an account of a traditional Kiowa storyteller. As the story would have been told aloud, the sentences are short, direct, simple, though laden with suggestive meaning.)

➤ Who do you think is the "Mooney" referred to at the end of the second account? (This is a historical account of Kiowa traditions told by an outsider to other outsiders.)

➤ Who is the "I" of the third account? (This is a youthful insider, perhaps Momaday himself. It is a story from his own childhood, a memoir.)

➤ How does reading these three very different accounts of the Tai-me affect your understanding of the story Momaday is telling? (Encourage students to think about how, although this method may at first seem confusing to the reader, it conveys a more accurate picture of the Tai-me than any one single voice would ever be able to accomplish.)

Writing

QUICK ASSESS

Do students' answers:

✔ describe the distinguishing characteristics of each storyteller?

✔ make a choice about which voice spoke most directly to them?

✔ explain why Momaday might choose to use multiple voices?

Students are asked to answer questions about the three accounts of the Tai-me. Invite students to share their understanding of who the three storytellers are before they proceed to analyze the accounts. On the board, chart the distinguishing characteristics of each speaker, with lines from the excerpt cited as evidence.

READING AND WRITING EXTENSIONS

➤ Have students identify a holiday that has cultural significance for their family (Christmas, Hanukah, Thanksgiving). Have them describe this day from the point of view of a small child, an adult, and an outsider.

➤ Ask students to research the Kiowa tribe, the Tai-me, and the ceremony of the Sun Dance and to report their findings as a fourth voice in this medley.

Four Fictionalizing Personal Experience

Critical Reading

FOCUS

Julia Alvarez explains her method of storytelling:

"What you find here are the Mirabals of my creation, made up but, I hope, true to the spirit of the real Mirabals."

BACKGROUND

Julia Alvarez was ten years old when her parents were forced to emigrate to the United States from the Dominican Republic. Her father had participated in a plot to overthrow the dictator, Raphael Trujillo. The plot was uncovered by Trujillo's secret police. *How the García Girls Lost Their Accents* is a chronicle of a family in exile that much resembles Alvarez's own experiences. In it, the García girls tell the story of how they came to be at home—and not at home—in America. Along with *How the García Girls Lost Their Accents*, Alvarez has written *In the Time of the Butterflies*, a fictionalized account of the 1960 murder of the Mirabal sisters by Trujillo. Julia Alvarez is currently a professor of English at Middlebury College in Vermont.

FOR DISCUSSION AND REFLECTION

➤ How were Yolanda's experiences in grade school like and unlike your own? (Student answers will vary. Urge students to identify the lines in the excerpt that give us information about Yolanda's school days.)

➤ What does the list of new words Yolanda was learning tell you about the priorities of her teacher? (Sister Zoe wants Yolanda to become familiar with what Sister sees as key elements of Yolanda's American life.)

➤ What does the second set of vocabulary words reveal about Sister Zoe? (She, like all adults during the Cuban Missile Crisis, was terrified of what would happen if diplomacy failed.)

➤ How is it possible that Yolanda would mistake snow for nuclear fallout? (Coming from the Dominican Republic, Yolanda had never seen snow before.)

Writing

QUICK ASSESS

Do students' fictional accounts:

✓ focus on a memorable moment in their lives?

✓ include a character to narrate the story?

Students are asked to write a fictionalized account of a moment from their own lives. Before they begin, have students reread the excerpt to identify techniques Alvarez uses to make her vignette come alive: dialogue, concrete details, irony, and humor.

READING AND WRITING EXTENSIONS

➤ Julia Alvarez's most recent novel, *Yo!*, continues the story of the García family. (Notice the irony of its title. "Yo" in Spanish means "I.") In it, Yolanda García's first highly autobiographical novel has met with great success in the outside world but outraged her family. Read students the prologue in which the sisters get their chance to tell the "truth" about Yo.

➤ Invite students to read "Making Up the Past" from Julia Alvarez's collection of poems *The Other Side*. This is another retelling of the story of her family's emigration. Have students compare these poems with "Snow."

Five Details Tell the Story

Critical Reading

FOCUS

From "How to Tell a True War Story":

"In a true war story, if there's a moral at all, it's like the thread that makes the cloth. You can't tease it out. You can't extract the meaning without unraveling the deeper meaning."

BACKGROUND

Tim O'Brien's collection of interrelated stories about the Vietnam War, *The Things They Carried*, is recognized as containing some of the best fiction about any war. O'Brien not only crystallizes the Vietnam experience, but he exposes the nature of all war stories. Richard Eder wrote, "These stories are memory as prophecy. They tell us not where we were but where we are, and perhaps where we will be. It is an ultimate, indelible image of war in our time, and in time to come." *The Things They Carried* was named as one of the best books of 1990 by the *New York Times Book Review*. The book of stories is bound together by O'Brien's own voice and character—that of a twenty-three-year-old foot soldier and that of a forty-three-year-old writer recreating that experience.

FOR DISCUSSION AND REFLECTION

➤ Why are war stories difficult ones to tell? (Answers will vary but should revolve around the difficulty of describing the horrors of war to those who were not there.)

➤ Why do you think O'Brien says that a true war story "never seems to end"? (Because the "characters" are often both unable to forget what they have experienced and unable to express fully how they feel about what they have seen, many war stories go on and on in a state of continuous revision.)

➤ What specific details about the Vietnam War in this excerpt made you feel that Tim O'Brien was telling the "truth" about war? (Responses will vary but may include "sitting in my foxhole, watching the shadows," and "how we would cross the river and march west.")

➤ What does O'Brien mean when he says that "A true war story, if truly told, makes the stomach believe"? What criteria do you use to determine if a story you hear is true or not? (Encourage students to speculate about what it means to feel in your gut that a story you have heard is not true.)

Writing

QUICK ASSESS

Do students' responses:

✓ reflect understanding of O'Brien's statement?

✓ offer their opinion on the effectiveness of abstractions?

Students are asked to write about what they think O'Brien means by this statement: "True war stories do not generalize. They do not indulge in abstraction or analysis." As a prewriting exercise, have students define the words *generalize*, *abstraction*, and *analysis*.

READING AND WRITING EXTENSIONS

➤ Have students choose an object from their backpacks or pockets—something that they typically carry—and write about what this object says about them. Why do they keep this object close? Then read together the title story from Tim O'Brien's collection *The Things They Carried*.

➤ Ask students to remember a time when someone told them a story they didn't believe. Have them write about how they felt and what, if anything, they said to the storyteller.

Unit Overview

"The Nonfiction Novel" introduces students to "new journalism." As they read and analyze excerpts from two nonfiction novels, *The Perfect Storm* and *Young Men and Fire*, they will explore how writers combine narrative techniques of fiction with the facts of journalistic reporting to produce powerful effects.

Literature Focus

	Lesson	Literature
1.	Working from Fact	**Norman Maclean,** from *Young Men and Fire* (Nonfiction)
2.	Cinematic Scenes	**Norman Maclean,** from *Young Men and Fire* (Nonfiction)
3.	Horizontal and Vertical Tellings	**Norman Maclean,** from *Young Men and Fire* (Nonfiction)
4.	Digressions	**Sebastian Junger,** from *The Perfect Storm* (Nonfiction)
5.	Recreating Experience	**Sebastian Junger,** from *The Perfect Storm* (Nonfiction)

Reading Focus

1. A good researcher presents the key facts. A good storyteller then uses the techniques of fiction to help add immediacy and dramatic effect to real-life situations.
2. Authors need to organize their information with concrete descriptions to help the reader see the scene.
3. Horizontal description provides information about what happened. Vertical description helps reveal the significance of the events and details.
4. Writers use digressions to provide readers with additional insight and meaning that cannot be revealed through the story or plot line.
5. Readers need to be aware of the differences between fact and conjecture when they interpret a nonfiction story.

Writing Focus

1. Analyze an author's use of fictional techniques.
2. Sketch two scenes of a nonfiction novel.
3. Complete a timeline of events for a scene, listing important details for each event.
4. Explain an author's use of digressions.
5. Write about the strengths and weaknesses of the nonfiction novel as a genre.

One Working from Fact

Critical Reading

FOCUS

The nonfiction novel is a book-length narrative about actual people and actual events written in the style of a novel.

BACKGROUND

Truman Capote insisted that *In Cold Blood* was not journalism but a new literary genre he had invented, "the nonfiction novel." Writers of this genre present a wealth of concrete detail — some observed, some imagined — and then allow readers to draw whatever moral seems appropriate. More like commentaries than documentaries, these works stimulate a powerful response in critical readers.

➤ In *Young Men and Fire*, Norman Maclean attempted to recreate what happened in 1949 when twelve smokejumpers lost their lives struggling with the Mann Gulch forest fire.

FOR DISCUSSION AND REFLECTION

➤ Why do you think Norman Maclean describes the geography of the area in such detail? (He wants readers who have never been to Montana or seen a forest fire to be able to visualize the scene in their minds.)

➤ How do the concrete details make the story Maclean tells more credible? (A reader can believe that the writer has been to this place as a careful observer and is reporting back what he has seen.)

➤ How do phrases such as "nature plays the leading role" and "the struggle between mountains and the plains" affect Maclean's report? (Answers will vary, but many students will say that this personification of nature helps them to engage imaginatively in what is being described.)

Writing

QUICK ASSESS

Do students' responses:

✔ distinguish Maclean's observations from his commentary?

✔ explain how Maclean achieves a dramatic effect?

Students are asked to describe how Maclean adds dramatic effect to the details his research has uncovered. As they reread the excerpt, have students underline passages in which they feel that Maclean has used the techniques of fiction writing to make the story come alive.

READING AND WRITING EXTENSIONS

➤ Encourage students to research smokejumping. Have them find out what qualifications are necessary for the job and share the information with the class.

➤ Have students read a nonfiction novel and report back to the class on what they learned about the "new journalism." Possible selections include *The Pump House Gang* by Tom Wolfe, *Paper Lion* by George Plimpton, *Armies of the Night* by Norman Mailer, *The Selling of the President* by Joe McGinnis, and *The Studio* by John Gregory Dunne.

TWOCinematic Scenes

C r i t i c a l   R e a d i n g

FOCUS

In the 1960s, writers with reputations as fine novelists turned to writing for newspapers and magazines in a style called the "new journalism," appropriating the techniques of fiction writing for the purpose of telling true stories.

BACKGROUND

Tom Wolfe asserted that the reason nonfiction writers turned to the new journalism was that readers were bored: "The voice of the narrator was one of the great problems in nonfiction writing. Most nonfiction writers, without knowing it, wrote in a century-old British tradition in which it was understood that the narrator shall assume a calm, cultivated and genteel voice. Readers were bored to tears without understanding why. When they came upon that pale beige tone, it signalled to them, unconsciously, that a well-known bore was here again, the journalist, a pedestrian mind, a phlegmatic spirit, a faded personality, and there was no way to get rid of the pallid little troll short of ceasing to read." (*The New Journalism*, 1973)

FOR DISCUSSION AND REFLECTION

➤ Why do you think Maclean chose to use the language of flowers ("a spot fire flowered," "tossed themselves as bouquets across the gulch," "a garden of wildfire") to describe a fire? (The writer uses images that are familiar to readers to describe what may otherwise be unfamiliar. While most of us have seen bouquets tossed and flowers blooming, not many of us have observed a forest fire.)

➤ Why do you think Maclean chooses to mix his metaphors? (A mixed metaphor is a figure of speech that combines two or more incongruous images. An example is Maclean's use of garden imagery and light bulbs in the same sentence. Maclean combines these disparate images to portray on the page what is happening to the landscape.)

➤ What picture did the phrase "left a world that is still burned out" create in your mind? (Answers should reflect the devastation a fire leaves in its wake.)

W r i t i n g

QUICK ASSESS

Do students' sketches:

✓ incorporate specific textual details?

✓ reflect an attempt to visualize what they read?

Students are asked to sketch the scene they see in their minds after reading the passage by Maclean. After they draw, have students identify the place in the excerpt that they illustrated. This will help them return to the spot for additional details.

READING AND WRITING EXTENSIONS

➤ *Hiroshima* (1946), by John Hersey, paved the way for journalistic novels like *Young Men and Fire*. This account of the World War II bombing of the Japanese city is told through the histories of six survivors. Divide the class into six groups and have each one read a section from *Hiroshima* and summarize it for the class.

➤ Ask students to look up forest fires in an encyclopedia or on the Internet. Have them write about how factual explanations are similar to and different from Norman Maclean's method of reporting.

Three Horizontal and Vertical Tellings

Critical Reading

FOCUS

Norman Maclean writes that "When all is said and done, we still accept the hands of Jim Harrison's watch, which were melted permanently at about four minutes to six, as marking approximately the time that the fire was catching up to the crew."

BACKGROUND

Traditional nonfiction is a literary genre consisting of news reports, feature articles, essays, editorials, textbooks, historical, and biographical works that describe or interpret facts and present judgments and opinions. The major goals of nonfiction prose are truth in reporting and logic in reasoning. In imaginative literature, the aim is truth to life and human nature; in nonfiction prose, the goal is truth to the factual world of news, science, and history. Writers of nonfiction novels have blurred the line dividing these two kinds of writing. They hold, at once, the seemingly contradictory goals of truth in reporting and truth to life. One method for achieving this involves the use of vertical tellings. Unlike traditional nonfiction in which a story unfolds in chronological order, proceeding from start to finish on a horizontal plane, nonfiction novels interrupt the narrative for musings by the author about the significance of events.

FOR DISCUSSION AND REFLECTION

➤ What do the references to time add to the story? (They lend an air of exactitude to Maclean's reporting; if he got such minute details down, the rest of what he describes must also be accurate.)

➤ Why do you think Maclean includes Jansson's descriptions of what happens to him physically? (These details—"cook out his lungs" and "I conked out from a lack of oxygen"—help the reader identify with Jansson's dilemma and suffering.)

➤ How did you interpret Jansson's short response to the question about what the fire looked like? (Student answers will vary, but by simply calling what happened "a blowup" and then saying no more, Jansson indicates that what he saw was a holocaust. He had no desire to elaborate.)

Writing

QUICK ASSESS

Do students' lists:

✓ identify key events on a timeline?

✓ list appropriate details for each event?

Students are asked to complete a timeline of events (horizontal telling) in Maclean's description of the blowout and then to list the details (vertical telling) he provides for the event.

READING AND WRITING EXTENSIONS

➤ Have students write a dialogue between a recruiter for the U.S. Forest Service and a young man or woman considering firefighting as a career. What questions might the Forest Service officer want to ask the recruit? What questions might the recruit have for the veteran?

➤ Read to students from Ralph Waldo Emerson's essay "Self-Reliance": "What I must do is all that concerns me, not what the people think. It is the harder because you will always find those who think they know what is your duty better than you know it." Ask students to speculate on what Jansson would think of Emerson's views of duty and self-reliance in light of his experience in the Mann Gulch.

Four Digressions

Critical Reading

FOCUS

Publishers were doubtful about how a book about a storm would sell.

"It looks like an unimportant topic," Junger has said. "But if you do it right, you can write about almost anything."

BACKGROUND

The *Andrea Gail,* a fishing boat from Massachusetts, was loaded with swordfish and a tired crew when, in October of 1991, it ran into what meteorologists have called "the perfect storm." Sebastian Junger's nonfiction novel *The Perfect Storm* tells the gripping story of the boat's fate as it confronts 100-foot waves and winds of more than 100 miles per hour. Junger details the working lives of sailors and life at sea as he reconstructs the boat's doomed trip. Using radio dialogues, published news accounts, and the testimony of eyewitnesses, Junger recreates in novelistic fashion the events of that fated day.

➤ The author makes use of digressions to offer readers related information about the fishing industry, the science of storms, and the lives of people who were changed forever by the storm. In this excerpt, Junger turns away from the chronological sequence of events, first to describe Bobby Shatford's inexplicable misgivings about this sailing and then to offer readers specific information about how storms are rated in the British *Manual of Seamanship.*

FOR DISCUSSION AND REFLECTION

➤ How did the description of Bobby Shatford's evening with Chris affect you as a reader? (Student answers will vary. The digression makes Bobby more real to us. His inexplicable fears remind us of those we all have felt at one time or another.)

➤ What does the extended quotation from the *Manual of Seamanship* add to the story? (This is information that readers who are not sailors are unlikely to possess. Junger offers it to us in order to make the news that the storm was Force 10 or 11 comprehensible.)

➤ How does the last line of this excerpt, "Very few boats that size can withstand a Force 12 gale," build suspense? (Readers begin to wonder if this storm will reach Force 12.)

Writing

QUICK ASSESS

Do students' explanations:

✓ accurately summarize two digressions?

✓ comment on their purpose in the story?

✓ analyze their effects on the reader?

Students are asked to summarize the two digressions in this excerpt, describe their purpose, and explain their effect. Before they begin to write, make a list on the board of possible purposes for digressions in storytelling.

READING AND WRITING EXTENSIONS

➤ Have students write an interior monologue for Chris, Bobby Shatford's girlfriend, as she sits listening to radio reports of the storm in which Bobby has been caught up.

➤ Read to students from one of Herman Melville's digressions on whaling in *Moby Dick* and ask them to compare Melville's technique with that of Junger.

Five Recreating Experience

Critical Reading

FOCUS

Dava Sobel writes, "Like victims of a perfect crime, readers of *The Perfect Storm* are first seduced into caring for the book's doomed characters, then compelled to watch them carried into the maw of a meteorological hell."

BACKGROUND

Writers of nonfiction novels develop the habit of staying with the people they were writing about for days and weeks at a time. They feel that they have to gather all the material the conventional journalist is after and more. It is important for them to be there when dramatic scenes took place, to get the dialogue, the gestures, the facial expressions, the details of the environment. As Tom Wolfe wrote in *The New Journalism*, "The idea was to give the full objective description, plus something that readers had always had to go to novels and short stories for: namely, the subjective or emotional life of the characters. That was why it was so ironic when both the journalistic and literary old guards began to attack this new journalism as being 'impressionistic.' Eventually I, and others, would be accused of 'entering people's minds.' But exactly! I figured that was one more doorbell a reporter had to push."

FOR DISCUSSION AND REFLECTION

➤ Can you identify places in this excerpt where Junger is obviously speculating about what might have happened? (In the second paragraph Junger imagines what might be going through one of the fisherman's minds. Junger has no evidence that this actually happened.)

➤ Do you believe that Junger is a reliable storyteller? (Answers will vary, but many students will say that the rich detail that Junger provides for the reader lends credibility to his story. Junger's tone is humble and probing. He never seems to demand that the reader take his word for what has happened.)

➤ What images from this excerpt are going to stay with you? (Student answers will vary.)

Writing

QUICK ASSESS

Do students' responses:

✓ identify the strengths and weaknesses of the nonfiction novel as a genre?

✓ see what might draw a writer to this form?

As students compose their responses to the nonfiction novel as a genre, encourage them to be skeptical. Discuss together what the dangers of such a genre might be and how these fictional techniques in the hands of an unscrupulous storyteller could lead readers astray.

READING AND WRITING EXTENSIONS

➤ Read the opening passage of Jon Krakauer's *Into Thin Air*, a first-hand account of an Everest expedition that ended in tragedy. Have students discuss why readers find stories about the struggle against the forces of nature so compelling.

➤ Ask students to underline particularly evocative or luminous phrases in these two excerpts from *The Perfect Storm* and arrange them on a page to form a found poem. Remind students that they may choose to repeat key words or phrases in their poem.

Unit Overview

"Seeing the Landscape" focuses on techniques writers use to convey a sense of place. By examining the details of the setting in several passages of nonfiction, students will deepen their understanding of how writers use descriptions of landscapes to reveal traits of their characters as well as their own personal values.

Literature Focus

Lesson	Literature
1. A Landscape of Beauty and Fear	**Ernie Pyle,** "Ahead of the Night" (Nonfiction)
2. Creating a Personal View	
3. Revealing Character	**Ted Conover,** from *Rolling Nowhere* (Nonfiction)
4. Landscape and Identity	**Annie Dillard,** from *Pilgrim at Tinker Creek* (Nonfiction)
5. Landscape and Values	**Jon Roush,** "Square Space" (Nonfiction)

Reading Focus

1. Authors employ sensory and emotional details to create a sense of a place. Understanding the meaning of a text requires understanding the author's personal view of the landscape.
2. Everyone has a personal view of places and events.
3. Active readers notice the details of setting, which authors use to enrich their description of a person's character.
4. Understanding how we observe our surroundings can reveal insights into who we are.
5. Sorting out the author's values is essential for understanding an argument.

Writing Focus

1. Use sensory details and comparisons to describe a place.
2. Create a personalized map of the United States.
3. Describe a person based on a description of her surroundings.
4. Explain how sight can lead to insight.
5. Write a letter to the author, explaining whether or not you agree with the main point of his essay.

One A Landscape of Beauty and Fear

C r i t i c a l   R e a d i n g

FOCUS

When describing a landscape, the writer shows the reader where things are located from both a physical and psychological perspective.

BACKGROUND

Descriptive writing portrays people, places, things, moments, and concepts with enough vivid detail to help the reader create a mental picture of what is being written about. In the excerpt "Ahead of the Night," Ernie Pyle takes his readers to unfamiliar territory. He appeals to the senses and lets readers see, smell, hear, taste, and feel what he felt during a blizzard in the Cumberland Mountains. Pyle first generically describes the experience of falling snow. Then he offers readers a geographical location for the snow storm. In the third passage, Pyle describes how it feels to stand in this Cumberland valley and look up at the snow beginning to fall. He goes on to explain what natives do when they look up and see such a sky, given their knowledge of what will follow. The final passage places the writer in this landscape. He is new to this scene, a "tenderfoot," and particularly sensitive to the feeling of fear that this snowstorm inspires.

FOR DISCUSSION AND REFLECTION

➤ How did the surroundings that Pyle describes remind you of other places where you have been? (Push students to think beyond instances of falling snow to landscapes where they have felt an indefinable fear.)

➤ What do you think Ernie Pyle wanted you to feel after reading "Ahead of the Night"? (Possible responses include a sense of awe in the presence of nature, a heightened awareness of falling snow, a desire to have been there with him.)

➤ Have students share the words and phrases that they found most evocative in the excerpt. Which descriptions made Pyle's experience come alive for you? (As students respond, ask them to try to explain why they think these particular words and phrases worked such magic on them as readers.)

W r i t i n g

QUICK ASSESS

Do students' descriptions:

✓ contain sensory details and/or comparisons?

✓ adopt a distinct point of view?

✓ convey a sense of place?

Students are asked to write a description that conveys a sense of place. Before they begin, have students decide what they want a reader to feel after reading their description.

READING AND WRITING EXTENSIONS

➤ Ask students to imagine Ernie Pyle as a poet instead of an essayist. Have them use words from "Ahead of the Night" to create the poem he might have written that night in a room of a little inn in a mountain village.

➤ Have students think of an unusual place they have visited and describe it by using comparisons that might help their readers visualize the scene.

Two Creating a Personal View

Critical Reading

FOCUS
Landscapes often reflect personal views.

BACKGROUND

Ernie Pyle is best known for his simple, descriptive stories about U.S. soldiers during World War II. His highly personal newspaper columns, like photographs, erased the war's abstractions. They zoomed in on the mud, the cold, the loneliness, and the inner thoughts of America's fighting men. Other journalists wrote from a wide-angle perspective. Pyle shot close-ups. Other war correspondents stayed safely back from the front and asked the boys how it was when they got back. Pyle would go right up there with them and dig his own foxhole. Ernie Pyle was killed in 1945 by a Japanese sniper's bullet while covering the war on the Pacific island of Ie Shima.

FOR DISCUSSION AND REFLECTION

➤ Ask students to look at the map of the United States and to refocus this wide-angle perspective of the country into a series of close-up photographs. Have students share what they see. (Accept descriptions of images that may have come from the movies or the news as well as those that come from students' own experiences.)

➤ Have students brainstorm a list of familiar places on the map (the Mississippi River, Florida vacationland, the Pacific beaches). Then for each location have students create a symbol that depicts a key feature of this place.

➤ Why do you think certain places elicit strong feelings? (Sometimes feelings result from personal experience, sometimes from a horrific news story, sometimes from photographs of natural disasters, sometimes from stories we have read or been told.)

Writing

QUICK ASSESS
Do students' maps:

✓ include a variety of pictures or symbols?

✓ convey a personal view of the United States?

Students are asked to create a personalized map of the United States in which their own experiences are portrayed. In order to prevent students who have never traveled from feeling at a loss, demonstrate on the board how one small town or corner of a big city could be the dominating image of the whole map. Another possible way students may interpret this exercise is to include on the map their preconceived notions of places like Hollywood, New England, New York, Death Valley, or the Middle West. If possible, bring in an atlas to help students locate places that they want to identify on their maps.

READING AND WRITING EXTENSIONS

➤ Have students imagine that they are on vacation in the place they would most like to visit. Suggest that they write a postcard home to their best friend describing what they have seen and how they felt.

➤ In *Blue Highways: A Journey Into America*, William Least Heat Moon describes a circular journey that he took across the United States. Like *Rolling Nowhere*, it is an impressionistic description of what the writer has seen, smelled, heard, tasted, and felt. Read from this travel memoir and have students compare Least Heat Moon's style with that of Ernie Pyle.

Three Revealing Character

Critical Reading

FOCUS

In *Rolling Nowhere*, Ted Conover describes the lives of people unlikely to have an entry in *Who's Who in America* and uses the setting to reveal their personalities.

BACKGROUND

Reading allows us to know people who might never otherwise cross our path but who are very much a part of the American landscape. Sheba is an example of such a character. Ted Conover traveled across the country talking to all kinds of individuals, recording their conversations and his impressions of the lives they are leading. In *Rolling Nowhere,* he offers readers rich detail about Americans who never make it into our history books.

➤ It may help students think about the sense of place in this piece if you locate Bakersfield on a map.

FOR DISCUSSION AND REFLECTION

➤ Why do you think Ted Conover used a description of the shack Sheba built to describe her character? (Details about Sheba's home reveal a great deal about her. She is ingenious, industrious, intrepid. These qualities are not often ascribed to a hobo and had Conover simply told us that Sheba possessed them, we are unlikely to have believed him.)

➤ Ted Conover's description of his meeting with Sheba is made up primarily of dialogue. How does this influence your interpretation of her character? (So much of what is revealed about her life comes to us in her own words that we trust Conover's portrayal.)

➤ Reread the passage, paying particular attention to Conover's questions. What is there about the manner of his questioning that might cause Sheba to reveal so much so freely? (His questions are short and nonjudgmental of her way of life and of the choices she has made. He seems to care about her welfare: "The trains are safer?")

Writing

QUICK ASSESS

Do students' descriptions:

✔ include accurate details of Sheba's appearance and habits?

✔ reflect an understanding of Sheba's character?

Students are asked to imagine that one of Sheba's sons wants to find her and to write a description that he might give to a private detective. Have students reread the excerpt, highlighting specific details about Sheba's appearance and habits. A detective will want information about how Sheba is different from all the other hobos out on the road.

READING AND WRITING EXTENSIONS

➤ Ask students to describe the details of the landscape that surround them. Have them picture themselves in a typical location—in a bedroom, on a street corner, on the soccer field — and write a description of themselves, using information about the setting to reveal aspects of their character.

➤ Read aloud from Chapter Three, "Homeboy," of *The Autobiography of Malcolm X.* Have students discuss how the setting of the streets in Roxbury, Boston, adds to readers' understanding of the young Malcolm X's character.

Four Landscape and Identity

Critical Reading

FOCUS

Annie Dillard on two ways to stalk the Divine:

"The first is not what you think of as true stalking. I put myself in the way of the creature's passage and wait, emptied. Stalking the other way, I forge my own passage seeking the creature. I wander the banks; what I find, I follow."

BACKGROUND

In her Pulitzer Prize-winning *Pilgrim at Tinker Creek*, Annie Dillard uses stories of her experiences living alone near Tinker Creek to write about the human condition. Her prose wraps you up in her own observations and makes you feel as though you are there with her. In this excerpt, Dillard reflects on the nature of seeing and how, for her, unless she makes herself pay attention to something in the landscape, she won't actually "see" it. She identifies this way of seeing as an analytical approach to seeing. But Dillard insists that there is another kind of seeing as well, the kind that "involves a letting go." She offers an example of this kind of seeing through a story about watching minnows.

FOR DISCUSSION AND REFLECTION

➤ How did reading this passage from *Pilgrim at Tinker Creek* make you feel? (Student answers will vary. Like a poem, Dillard's writing can be perplexing at first. With careful rereading, her meaning opens up to the reader.)

➤ Why do you think Annie Dillard makes reference to Thoreau? (Henry David Thoreau believed that humankind should learn to live simply and organically, returning to nature in a kind of natural mysticism. Dillard's advice to us about seeing is similar to that of Thoreau.)

➤ Explain Dillard's reference to the man watching a baseball game. ("Like a blind man at a baseball game," Dillard says that she needs radio commentary to make sense of what she sees when operating from an analytical stance. Without words, she won't pay attention to what is before her. Dillard compares seeing by "letting go" to a man watching a baseball game in silence in an empty stadium: "I see the game purely; I'm abstracted and dazed." This is a Thoreau-like way of seeing.)

Writing

QUICK ASSESS

Do students' responses:

✓ draw on specifics from the texts?

✓ refer to personal experiences?

✓ explain how sight can lead to insight?

Students are asked to explain how sight can lead to insight. Before they begin writing, ask for volunteers to share examples from their own lives in which the observation of a detail in the landscape has caused them to reflect on larger issues.

READING AND WRITING EXTENSIONS

➤ Barry Lopez is another nature writer who uses sight to lead to insight. Encourage students to read from his book *Arctic Dreams: Imagination and Desire in a Northern Landscape* and compare Lopez's methods of landscape description with that of Annie Dillard.

➤ All accomplished naturalists and nature writers learn to take field notes. Have students take a pen and a pad of paper on a walk to a secluded spot and record everything they see, hear, smell, touch, and feel as they sit and observe the natural world around them.

Five Landscape and Values

Critical Reading

FOCUS

Understanding why Jon Roush asks us to consider the landscape from the bison's point of view means understanding his personal values.

BACKGROUND

Jon Roush takes an event in Montana's Bitterroot Valley—a bison wandering away from home—and uses this occurrence to reflect upon the nature of holding the wilderness in protective custody. One "unnatural" feature of our state parks is that their borders are drawn according to a grid pattern, often with little attention to the shape of the land. Roush uses the absurdity of expecting a bison to see the logic of such borders to warn us about what we have lost in the process of exerting logical control over nature. "A fully civilized life includes more than law and order," writes Roush. "It includes mystery, diversity, surprise, and beauty—the qualities that make natural space nourishing and occasionally dangerous."

FOR DISCUSSION AND REFLECTION

➤ How does knowing that Jon Roush is president of the environmental protection group Wilderness Society influence your reading of this essay? (That biographical information provides a clue to the writer's perspective on wilderness development and helps readers understand his point of view.)

➤ Why is Roush's strategy of inviting the reader to view the landscape from the point of view of the bison effective? (He asks the reader to see the landscape through a different set of eyes. Suddenly things we take for granted—for example, roads laid out in a grid pattern without reference to the natural landscape—seem absurd.)

➤ What do you think Jon Roush wanted the reader to think after reading his essay? (Reponses will vary. Roush wants to sensitize readers to the integrity of the wilderness and to see what we have lost by the "fragmentation of western space.")

Writing

QUICK ASSESS

Do students' letters:

✔ identify Jon Roush's point of view in "Square Space"?

✔ clearly state their opinion of Roush's point?

✔ use examples to clarify their values?

Students are instructed to write a letter to Jon Roush explaining whether they agree or disagree with him. On the board, review the conventions of such a formal letter.

READING AND WRITING EXTENSIONS

➤ In a curious postscript, twelve years after preventing a timber cut on federal land adjacent to his own property, Jon Roush logged off an 80-acre patch of old-growth forest on his $2.5 million Bitterroot Valley, Montana, ranch. Roush claims the logging was part of a separation agreement with his wife. For details, have students read "Wilderness Society President in Chainsaw Massacre on His Own Land," EnviroNews Service (newsdesk@envirolink.org) and summarize their findings for the class.

➤ Have students research the life and ideas of architect Frank Lloyd Wright and the "Prairie School" of architecture he developed based on his views of the flat midwestern land.

U n i t   O v e r v i e w

In this unit, students consider the topic of the American Dream from several perspectives. As they read and respond to a variety of poetry and nonfiction, they will examine how authors define a subject, develop it with symbols, use satire, and force readers to examine their own assumptions.

L i t e r a t u r e   F o c u s

	Lesson	**Literature**
1.	Defining the Dream	**Anzia Yezierska,** from "America and I" (Nonfiction)
		Joseph Bruchac, "Ellis Island" (Poetry)
2.	Defining a Subject Through Symbols	
3.	Examining Assumptions	**Sherman Alexie,** "Translated from the American" (Poetry)
4.	Satirizing the Subject	**E. E. Cummings,** "next to of course god america i" (Poetry)
5.	Reporting an Incident	**Joan Didion,** from "Where the Kissing Never Stops" (Nonfiction)

R e a d i n g   F o c u s

1. An author's definition of a subject shapes the way he or she writes about it.
2. When writers use symbols to develop a subject, they call upon the reader to supply additional meanings.
3. Authors challenge our assumptions about a subject in order to enlarge our understanding of it.
4. A satirical perspective on a subject reveals facets that, according to the author, should be changed.
5. Some subjects are developed through the way that an incident is presented. The writer reveals his or her views through choices about how an incident is told.

W r i t i n g   F o c u s

1. Explain contrasting perspectives in a poem.
2. Create a symbol to define the American Dream.
3. Explain a poet's use of irony.
4. Compose a satiric sonnet, modeled on an E. E. Cummings poem.
5. Write about how an author reveals her views through the way she presents an incident.

One Defining the Dream

Critical Reading

FOCUS

Newcomers to this country wonder, "Who am I? What am I? What do I want with my life? Where is America?"

BACKGROUND

In the late nineteenth century, there was great social upheaval in the United States. Entrepreneurs such as Andrew Carnegie, Henry Du Pont, and John D. Rockefeller amassed fortunes by exploiting cheap labor in the cities. Much of this workforce was made up of immigrants in search of a better life. Both the industrialists and the immigrants possessed dreams. For the 23 million immigrants who came to America between 1881 and 1920, the American Dream was not only a compelling idea but also a last chance at survival. Many were escaping famine or persecution in their homelands; they sought in this country a new life for themselves and for their children. Anzia Yezierska's account of disillusion and persistence offers readers a picture of what the American Dream felt like for immigrants in the sweatshops of New York City's garment district.

➤ Help students understand Bruchac's poem by discussing Ellis Island, the first stop for many immigrants who came to the United States in the late 1800s and early 1900s. There, immigrants were examined and either admitted or deported.

FOR DISCUSSION AND REFLECTION

➤ How does the first-person point of view in "America and I" affect you as a reader? (This kind of narration most often causes a reader to sympathize with the story being told.)

➤ Based upon this excerpt, how would you define the American Dream that Anzia Yezierska's narrator holds in her heart? (Answers will vary but should reflect an awareness of her optimism and hopes for a better life in the New World.)

➤ Students who are new to this country may identify with Anzia Yezierska's experience. If they feel comfortable doing so, invite them to share what their families have learned since coming to this country.

➤ How does the dream described in Joseph Bruchac's poem differ from the narrator's in "America and I"? (Bruchac speaks not only for the new arrivals to this country but also for the Native Americans who have been displaced.)

Writing

QUICK ASSESS

Do students' explanations:

✓ identify both the immigrant and Native American perspectives?

✓ show the complexity of this thing called the "American Dream"?

Students are asked to analyze the idea of the American Dream in "Ellis Island," describing the contrasting perspectives of immigrants from Europe and Native Americans. Before they write, invite students to think about how different peoples can want different things from their country.

READING AND WRITING EXTENSIONS

➤ Later in Anzia Yezierska's memoir she writes, "Who am I? What am I? What do I want with my life? Where is America? Is there an America? What is this wilderness in which I'm lost?" Have students try answering these questions for themselves and for their own lives.

➤ Ask students to read the whole of "America and I" to discover how the narrator's perspective on the American Dream shifts as reality sets in.

Two Defining a Subject Through Symbols

Critical Reading

FOCUS

Symbols carry powerful condensed meanings; that is their function.

BACKGROUND

Joseph Bruchac is a master storyteller and writer of Abenaki, English, and Slovak ancestry. While studying at Cornell, Bruchac decided to take a writing class. "I always loved to write," he remembers, "even though I was in the school of agriculture majoring in Wildlife Conservation. Three weeks into the class my instructor said, 'Give it up. You'll never write a good poem.' From that point on, I literally ate, slept, and dreamt poetry."

➤ In his poem "Ellis Island," Bruchac works with the symbol of the Statue of Liberty, ". . . the island / of the tall woman, green / as dreams of forests and meadows / waiting for those who'd worked / a thousand years / yet never owned their own."

➤ Usually a symbol functions as a kind of force field sending out waves of suggestion that penetrate many layers of a poem or story and add to its meaning. It is not so much to be identified as to be probed and questioned. Encourage students to think about what the following symbols suggest to them: a flying bird, a crushed flower, a gun, a watch, a knife. Remind them that sometimes a flying bird symbolizes freedom, and sometimes it is simply a flying bird.

FOR DISCUSSION AND REFLECTION

➤ Name a few famous Americans and ask students what kind of symbols they think these individuals would choose to represent their version of the American Dream.

➤ What does the Statue of Liberty symbolize for you? What is there about the statue that you think may have caused it to become a powerful symbol for so many Americans? (Answers will vary, especially depending upon students' familiarity with the statue and the history of immigration.)

Writing

QUICK ASSESS

Do students' symbols:

✔ represent their own idea of the American Dream?

✔ include words that describe their view?

Students are asked to create their own symbol to define the American Dream and to write words that are associated with their view of it. Some students may wish to begin with the words, others with an image. Assure them that what matters is their idea, not their artistry or lack thereof.

READING AND WRITING EXTENSIONS

➤ Have students research the history of the Statue of Liberty and present what they have discovered to the class.

➤ Invite students to research Ellis Island—what it was like in the early twentieth century and what it is like now.

Three Examining Assumptions

Critical Reading

FOCUS

Sherman Alexie has said that he grew up with discrimination:

"It is with me in my life. I can't turn it off."

BACKGROUND

Poets often create ironic effects by playing against the reader's expectations. In "Translated from the American," Sherman Alexie contrasts the stereotypes of Native Americans most Americans have formed from watching old movies with the realities of contemporary Native American life. Sherman Alexie has said in an interview that "Most of my heroes are just decent people. Decency is rare and underrated. I think my writing is somehow just about decency. Still, if I was keeping score, and I like to keep score, I would say the villains in the world are way ahead of the heroes. I hope my writing can help even the score."

➤ Alexie is a Spokane, Coeur d'Alene from Willipinit, Washington. His prose and poetry are filled with passion and affection yet echo with the irony, anger, and pain of reservation life.

FOR DISCUSSION AND REFLECTION

➤ What examples can you find of Alexie's playing with stereotypical images of Indians? (Answers include "I'll make camp," "wrap myself / in old blankets," "watch this Indian / speak in subtitles," "surround me," and "ask 'how.'")

➤ What references within the poem let you know that the "I" in this poem is a thoroughly modern narrator? (Students may mention "after all the drive-in movies have closed" or "where I keep / a post office box.")

➤ How would you describe this narrator's version of the American Dream? (Responses should reflect an awareness of the narrator's status in society.)

➤ Why do you think Alexie identifies his poem as "Translated from the American"? (The traditional American version of confrontations between white men and Native Americans ends with the white man on top. Alexie is determined to "replay" this version of the old story.)

Writing

QUICK ASSESS

Do students' explanations:

✓ comment on the irony?

✓ examine how readers are forced to examine their assumptions about Native Americans?

✓ reveal a thoughtful reading of the poem?

Students are asked to write an explanation of Alexie's use of irony in "Translated from the American." Begin by asking them to think about other places where they find the expression "translated from" and to consider what Alexie is saying about the poem that follows when he identifies it as a "translation."

READING AND WRITING EXTENSIONS

➤ Read aloud other poems of Sherman Alexie's from his collection *The Business of Fancy Dancing*. Have students find examples of irony in these poems.

➤ Have students write about a time when they feel that they have been stereotyped or judged on the basis of what they look like rather than on the basis of who they are inside.

Four Satirizing the Subject

Critical Reading

FOCUS

Cummings often satirized American culture, believing that mankind was at times cruel, stupid, and even self-destructive, but he never shunted responsibility for the world's failure away from individuals. We created this mess. No one but us is likely to clean it up.

BACKGROUND

E.E. Cummings is highly regarded for his prose as well as his poetry. Influenced by his experiences as an ambulance driver in France during World War I, he wrote *The Enormous Room.* Rarely taught in high school, it is a remarkable companion piece to Eric Maria Remarque's *All Quiet on the Western Front.* Though Cummings' poems appear complex, they most often offer a simple view of life. In an age dominated by Communism and materialism, Cummings urged readers to preserve and celebrate their individuality. Wordplay is a common feature in Cummings' poetry. In "next to of course god america I," wordplay allows him to satirize patriotism through the use of patriotic song lyrics.

FOR DISCUSSION AND REFLECTION

➤ What effect do the words "'and so forth'" have when sandwiched between "'land of the pilgrims'" and "'oh / say can you see by the dawn's early'"? (Cummings treats irreverently these phrases that have been enshrined in most Americans' minds as synonymous with freedom and liberty.)

➤ How would you paraphrase the line "'thy sons acclaim your glorious name by gorry / by jingo by gee by gosh by gum'"? (Student responses should address the nature of war, that act of ultimate patriotism. Explain, if students do not know, that jingoism is an aggressive attitude combining patriotism and contempt for other countries. The line is a collection of phrases popular with some people in the early part of this century. A current equivalent might be "darn right" or "you can bet on it.")

➤ Who do you think is the "He" of the final line? And why would "He" need a drink of water? (The sonnet satirizes the patriotic spirit that sends young men, "'heroic happy dead,'" out to die. The speaker may be a politician making a speech.)

Writing

QUICK ASSESS

Do students' sonnets:

✓ imitate Cummings's style?

✓ focus on an appropriate topic?

✓ use the standard sonnet rhyme scheme?

Students are asked to imitate Cummings's style in a satirical sonnet of their own. To help them begin, have students put the subject they plan to satirize in the center of a page and then create a cluster of words and phrases they associate with this idea all around it.

READING AND WRITING EXTENSIONS

➤ Have students bring in the words to the songs Cummings refers to and read or sing them in counterpoint to the poem.

➤ Ask students to write a poem of their own which borrows the words from patriotic songs to express their version of the American Dream. Suggest that they look back at the symbol they drew in Lesson Two for ideas.

Five Reporting an Incident

Critical Reading

FOCUS

Joan Didion explains that "I write entirely to find out what I'm thinking, what I'm looking at, what I see and what it means. What I want and what I fear."

BACKGROUND

"Where the Kissing Never Stops" is written in an understated style. Joan Didion never boldly offers her opinion of what she observes but instead carefully piles up descriptive details that invite the reader to draw conclusions. Joan Didion was born into a stable family with traditional values. Many of her columns and essays focus on the cultural changes and rebellion of the 1960s, the decade of Joan Baez's peak popularity.

FOR DISCUSSION AND REFLECTION

➤ Why do you think Didion gives readers details of the zoning code Joan Baez had allegedly violated? (By citing Section 32-C of the Monterey County Zone Code, Didion emphasizes that this was an actual court case, with legal repercussions for all parties. While making sure you have all the "facts," the author leaves analysis of the proceedings up to the reader.)

➤ How did learning that Mrs. Petkuss was "a plump young matron with an air of bewildered determination . . . in a strawberry-pink knit dress" influence your attitude towards her complaint about Miss Baez? (Student answers should reflect an awareness of how specific words can create tone and express an attitude.)

➤ What assumptions has Mrs. Petkuss made about what happens on the Baez property? (Because Joan Baez is a famous liberal and freethinker, Mrs. Petkuss imagines all kinds of violations of her idea of decency.)

➤ Why do you think Didion chooses not to reveal the outcome of this lawsuit in the beginning? (The outcome is not the author's concern. What she is concerned about is making the reader reflect upon how self-interest often determines individual's values. Later in the essay, she mentions that Baez's school was allowed to keep operating by a 3-2 vote of the Board of Supervisors.)

Writing

QUICK ASSESS

Do students' explanations:

✓ suggest how a writer's choice of details can reveal an attitude towards the subject?

✓ identify whose side Didion is on?

Students are asked to decide whose side Joan Didion seems to be taking in her article and to support their views with evidence from the essay. Begin by having students underline words and phrases from the text that demonstrate Didion's attitude toward events as they occurred.

READING AND WRITING EXTENSIONS

➤ Read passages from *The White Album*, Joan Didion's acclaimed collection of essays and have students respond to her ideas. For example, in "The Women's Movement," Didion writes, "One oppressed class after another had seemed finally to miss the point. The have-nots, it turned out, aspired mainly to having."

➤ Have students describe a period in one of their other classes. This should not be a description of a typical day but rather of one particular day in class. Remind them to employ all of their senses in recreating the scene for readers as Didion has done in her essay.

OBSERVING AND REFLECTING

U n i t   O v e r v i e w

In "Observing and Reflecting," students immerse themselves in poems by Robert Frost, Sylvia Plath, Jane Kenyon, Karl Shapiro, and Wallace Stevens. As they explore the ways in which poets observe, describe, and reflect on small, deceptively simple events and experiences, students will enhance their understanding and enjoyment of poetry.

L i t e r a t u r e   F o c u s

	Lesson	Literature
1.	Reflecting on a Small Event	**Robert Frost,** "Dust of Snow" (Poetry)
2.	Philosophical Reflections	**Sylvia Plath,** "Black Rook in Rainy Weather" (Poetry)
3.	Deceptively Simple	**Jane Kenyon,** "Otherwise" (Poetry)
4.	The Poet as Reporter	**Karl Shapiro,** "Auto Wreck" (Poetry)
5.	The Poet as Painter	**Wallace Stevens,** "Study of Two Pears" (Poetry)

R e a d i n g   F o c u s

1. Poets' observations of simple, everyday events often provide subjects for their poems.
2. In reading a philosophical poem, it is helpful to keep in mind the initial observation that inspired the poem.
3. Some poems seem simple on the surface, but have deeper meanings. Poets may signal these meanings by using a refrain that takes on new meaning by the end of the poem.
4. Like journalists, poets must observe, select, and present. At the end of the "broadcast," they, too, very often include a reflective comment.
5. Poets must observe the objects of their study as closely as scientists do. Close study enhances the believability of conclusions and reflections.

W r i t i n g   F o c u s

1. Write a poem based on a model.
2. Rewrite a poem to create an extended reflection on an event.
3. Create a poem using a refrain.
4. Recast the events of a poem as a news story.
5. Explain and react to a poem's closing lines.

One Reflecting on a Small Event

Critical Reading

FOCUS

Robert Frost once said, "One thing I care about is taking poetry as the first form of understanding. If poetry isn't understanding all, the whole world, then it isn't worth anything."

BACKGROUND

Robert Frost was a brilliant teacher. He had many valuable and pragmatic ideas about the imaginative act, the rush of inspiration, the methods of revision, and the pressures of publication. He was not a tormented, self-destructive poet—like Berryman, Lowell, or Plath—but one who loved the play of the imagination, took joy in his creation, and believed that "poetry spoils you for anything else in life." One of Frost's convictions was that the rhythm of human feeling should contend with the fixed rhythmic patterns of verse. Holding an almost mystical view of the power of metaphor, he contended that "Like a piece of ice on a hot stove, a poem must ride on its own melting." Robert Frost won the Pulitzer Prize for poetry four times. He died in Boston in 1963 at the age of 88.

FOR DISCUSSION AND REFLECTION

➤ Ask students to draw a sketch of the scene that they picture in their minds' eyes when they read this poem. Compare these images and discuss their differences.

➤ What does the narrator of this poem mean when he says that the dust of snow "saved some part / of a day I had rued"? (The small occurrence of a crow shaking snow from a branch broke the narrator's melancholy mood and made valuable what had been up until then a miserable day. *Rue* means to repent or regret.)

➤ How does the form of the poem, with its short lines, simple rhyme scheme, and small words, reinforce its message? (The poem is a reflection upon how the smallest thing can, if attended to, shift our perspective on the world. Frost conveys this idea with great economy in the tiny poem "Dust of Snow.")

Writing

QUICK ASSESS

Do students' poems:

✓ imitate Frost's form?

✓ describe the event?

✓ explain their feelings?

Students are asked to write a poem modeled after the one by Frost that is based upon an event in their lives. Have them choose an inconsequential, commonplace moment—perhaps an event that happened on the day they are writing—and see what happens as they conjure with this small, everyday occurrence.

READING AND WRITING EXTENSIONS

➤ Read students Robert Frost's enormously popular "Nothing Gold Can Stay" and ask students to compare its ruminative tone with that of "Dust of Snow."

➤ Have students write about a day they "rued" and what it was that brought them out of their bad mood.

Two Philosophical Reflections

Critical Reading

FOCUS
For Sylvia Plath, "The poets I delight in are as possessed by their poems as by the rhythms of their own breathing."

BACKGROUND
Sylvia Plath wrote confessional poetry—autobiographical poems that deal with personal issues and reveal details from the author's own life. In "Black Rook in Rainy Weather," she takes the inconsequential experience of watching a rook "ordering its black feathers" and uses that moment to ruminate upon her own inner landscape. The opening stanzas portray a cynical speaker who doesn't expect much from the world around her: "Although, I admit, I desire, / Occasionally, some backtalk / From the mute sky, I can't honestly complain: / A certain minor light may still / Leap incandescent." The rook "rearranging its feathers in the rain" was just such backtalk that caused her suddenly to pay attention to something outside herself.

➤ Certain words in this poem may pose challenges for students. Check that they understand the meanings of *desultory*, *portent*, *incandescent*, *obtuse*, *hallowing*, *largesse*, *ruinous*, *respite*, *trekking* and *spasmodic*.

FOR DISCUSSION AND REFLECTION
➤ Compare Plath's lines "Thus hallowing an interval / Otherwise inconsequent" with Frost's lines "saved some part / Of a day I had rued." (Both pairs of lines reflect upon how a small, seemingly unimportant event in the natural world can suddenly alter one's perspective.)

➤ What evidence do you find in the poem of the narrator's state of mind? (Students may mention "I now walk / Wary . . . /skeptical," "A brief respite from fear / Of total neutrality," "Trekking stubborn through this season / Of fatigue . . . ." The narrator seems obsessed with her own internal malaise.)

➤ In your opinion does the poem end on a positive or negative note? (Answers will vary. Plath says, however, that "Miracles occur." Even though one must often wait a long time "For that rare, random descent," it does happen.)

Writing

QUICK ASSESS
Do students' poems:
✓ imitate Plath's form?
✓ creatively reflect on the event's meaning?

Students are asked to take the same event that they used in writing a poem modeled after "Dust of Snow" as the subject of a second poem, this time modeled after "Black Rook in Rainy Weather." In order to help students stretch the ideas in their lean, spare poems into an extended reflection, have them talk with a classmate about why this event seemed worth writing about.

READING AND WRITING EXTENSIONS
➤ Read students Sylvia Plath's poem "Mirror" and discuss together how the personified mirror allows Plath to reflect upon the ways in which people look at themselves.

➤ Using the ideas from their poems, have students write a reflective essay on the subject of how small moments can offer insight.

Three Deceptively Simple

Critical Reading

FOCUS

Poetry can attain a density of meaning that we seldom encounter in prose. We are simultaneously affected by the meaning, word sound, and rhythm.

BACKGROUND

Poetry was once viewed as the most vital and important of the arts. The poet was a seer, a visionary, a dispenser of the secret wisdom of a culture. In her poem "Otherwise," Jane Kenyon (1947–1995) takes up the role of a wise one, warning readers that as we go about our commonplace, everyday, pleasurable tasks, not only could they "have been otherwise" but that one day they "will be otherwise." Along with its power to teach, poetry has the power to bring pleasure—the pleasure of rhythm and repetition and of sounds arranged in patterns. Jane Kenyon provides her readers with a refrain that both pleases the ear and challenges the status quo. Samuel Taylor Coleridge once defined poetry as "the best words in the best order." Kenyon's words are a model of the fusion between sound and sense while her "best order" purposefully throws the reader off balance.

FOR DISCUSSION AND REFLECTION

➤ Did Kenyon's first line "I got out of bed" make you want to read on, or did it seem too ordinary to be bothered with? (Student answers will vary, but help students to see that Kenyon may have written such a seemingly dull first line on purpose.)

➤ Why do you think Kenyon chose to break her line "It might have been otherwise" in so many different ways? (The unexpected line breaks keep the reader off-balance and moving quickly down the poem. Notice how the final anchor line "it will be otherwise" is left intact.)

➤ How does the final line make you feel? Depressed? Hopeless? Hopeful? Is this last line a trick? (Many responses are possible. And, yes, it is a bit of a trick on the part of the poet who wants the reader to reassess everything that has gone before.)

Writing

QUICK ASSESS

Do students' poems:

✓ describe several routine activities?

✓ use spare, simple statements?

Students are asked to write a poem of their own that uses Jane Kenyon's refrain "It might have been otherwise" as a vehicle to examine their own daily acts. Insisting that students keep the lines of their poems short will help them describe events as bare statements the way Kenyon has done.

READING AND WRITING EXTENSIONS

➤ Jane Kenyon died in April 1995. Her husband, poet Donald Hall, wrote a series of poems, called *Without,* about the woman who suffered and died, the doctors and nurses who tried but failed to save her, the friends who grieved for her, and the husband who sat by her while she lived and afterward sat alone. Read students a few poems from this collection.

➤ Have students write a poetry review of Jane Kenyon's poem "Otherwise" for their school newspaper. Why do they think other students would or wouldn't like this poem?

Four The Poet as Reporter

C r i t i c a l   R e a d i n g

FOCUS
Karl Shapiro's powers of observation and reflection are evident in *V-Letter and Other Poems,* for which he won the Pulitzer Prize for poetry in 1945.

BACKGROUND
Poetry is an uncommon medium for news reporting, but as Karl Shapiro's poem demonstrates, it can be an effective one for conveying not only the *who, what, where, when, why,* and *how* of an event but also the *what if, why not,* and *whatever for.* The event Shapiro describes is an automobile accident as observed through the eyes of a bystander. The narrator focuses first on the noise and lights that attract him to the scene, both of which are quickly attributed to the speeding ambulance, that "little hospital" where "the mangled" are "lifted / And stowed." In the second stanza the narrator observes policemen taking care of business after the accident: sweeping up glass, taking notes, washing away the blood, hanging warning lights on the wrecks. The third stanza uses the language of injury, "Our throats were tight as tourniquets / Our feet were bound with splints but now, / like convalescents," to describe how the bystanders felt as they stood at the scene of this accident. Normal traffic moves around the accident, but the witnesses stand transfixed by what they have seen. In the final paragraphs the narrator poses the existential question "Who shall die?"

FOR DISCUSSION AND REFLECTION
➤ Reread the first two stanzas of "Auto Wreck" and determine what you can tell from these lines about the accident. (It was a multi-car crash with bloody injuries.)

➤ Why do you think the bystanders' "throats were tight as tourniquets" and their "feet were bound with splints"? (Student answers will vary. The shock of what the bystanders have seen seems to immobilize them as though they must pause to reflect before they can resume their everyday lives.)

➤ According to Shapiro, how is death by auto wreck different from death by war, suicide, or cancer? (The causes for these deaths are identifiable while an accident "invites the occult mind" because it leaves us puzzled with only the "wicked stones" to blame.)

W r i t i n g

QUICK ASSESS
Do students' reports:
✓ translate the poem's story into prose?
✓ contain enough factual details?

Students are asked to rewrite Shapiro's poetic portrayal of this accident as a news reporter might. Put the words any news story must answer on the board to remind students of what will need to be added: *who, what, where, when, why,* and *how.*

READING AND WRITING EXTENSIONS
➤ Have students watch the evening news and then write a poem based on one of the day's stories to share with the class.

➤ Bring in newspapers and have students choose a story that intrigues them. Then ask them to underline interesting words and phrases from the article and rearrange them into a found poem. Suggest that students use the same title as the original story.

Five The Poet as Painter

Critical Reading

FOCUS

Randall Jarrell describing Wallace Stevens:

"If he were an animal, he would be, without a doubt, that rational, magnanimous, voluminous animal, the elephant."

BACKGROUND

In Wallace Stevens's "Study of Two Pears," the poet describes the fruit with the eyes of a painter. After citing the scientific name for pears, Stevens explains what the pears are not: "not viols, / Nudes or bottles. / They resemble nothing else." He then goes on to define their shape, "Composed of curves / Bulging toward the base," and their color, "The yellow glistens. / It glistens with various yellows, / Citrons, oranges and greens." While most poets revel in simile, Stevens insists that the pears "resemble nothing else." He demands that the reader experience the pears exactly as they sit on the green cloth, without recourse to comparison or metaphor.

FOR DISCUSSION AND REFLECTION

➤ Do you think a person who read only stanzas II through V would be able to guess what Stevens is describing? (Suggest that students experiment tonight with someone at home. Remember not to reveal the title of the poem.)

➤ What effect does the numbering of the stanzas have on you as a reader? (Many responses are possible. The Roman numerals add a sense of order and formal organization to the poem. Visually they separate the stanzas even further from one another—more than a traditional extra line would do.)

➤ How does the title "Study of Two Pears" prepare you for the lines of poetry which follow? ("Study of" is a common way to title a drawing or painting.)

Writing

QUICK ASSESS

Do students' explanations:

✓ explicate the final two lines of this poem?

✓ refer to specific textual details?

Students are asked to explain what they think Stevens means when he writes, "The pears are not seen / As the observer wills." Before students begin writing, show them an ordinary pencil and discuss how its color, shape, and form are independent of our view of the object. Unless the viewer chooses to break the pencil in half, his "will" does not shape it.

READING AND WRITING EXTENSIONS

➤ Read students Jane Kenyon's poem "The Pear" and have them compare her poetic use of the fruit with that of Wallace Stevens. Its last stanza reads, "It happens subtly, as when a pear / spoils from the inside out, / and you may not be aware / until things have gone too far."

➤ Bring in two fruits or vegetables and set them out in front of the class as a still life on a cloth. Have students write a poem of their own inspired by what they see. Invite them to paint with their words and share their creations.

EVALUATING POEMS

Unit Overview

In this unit, students explore the process of evaluating poetry. As they read and respond to poetry by Josephine Miles, Louise Glück, John Updike, and Carolyn Kizer, students will develop an appreciation of a poet's use of diction and sentiment and strengthen their abilities to establish appropriate criteria with which to judge the poems they read.

Literature Focus

	Lesson	Literature
1.	Establishing Criteria	**Josephine Miles,** "Sisyphus" (Poetry)
2.	Applying the Criteria	**Louise Glück,** "The Mountain" (Poetry)
3.	Comparing Two Poems	
4.	Sentiment and Sentimentality	**John Updike,** "Dog's Death" (Poetry)
5.	Precise Diction	**Carolyn Kizer,** "The Great Blue Heron" (Poetry)

Reading Focus

1. Evaluating the effectiveness of a poem in terms of one criterion provides a start toward building an interpretation.
2. Applying the same criterion to two poems is the basis for a comparison of the two poems.
3. Comparing two poems gives you the opportunity to make valid judgments based on selected criteria.
4. When judging a poem's use of sentiment, as opposed to sentimentality, a good reader looks at the poet's language. Concrete language with specific detail creates stronger emotional responses than flowery, overblown abstractions.
5. Precise diction is one of the most important characteristics of a good poem.

Writing Focus

1. Interpret a poem and evaluate its effectiveness.
2. Interpret a poem and evaluate its effectiveness.
3. Compare two poems based on selected criteria.
4. Explain whether a poem is sentimental.
5. Evaluate the effectiveness of a poem's diction.

One Establishing Criteria

C r i t i c a l   R e a d i n g

FOCUS

Before we can judge a poem's effectiveness, we need to set up criteria.

BACKGROUND

Sisyphus, a legendary king of Corinth, was reputed to be the most cunning man alive. When a neighbor stole Sisyphus's cattle and changed their appearance, Sisyphus was able to pick out his own, having marked them under their hoofs. When Death came to take him, the crafty Sisyphus chained Death up so that nobody died until Ares came and released him. For misdeeds on earth, Sisyphus was condemned in Hades to roll to the top of a hill a large stone, which, when it reached the summit, rolled down again; thus, his punishment was eternal.

➤ Helicon is a mountain in Boeotia, regarded as sacred to the Muses.

➤ The last lines of the third stanza are a reference to Robert Browning's lines, "Ah, but a man's reach should exceed his grasp, / Or what's a heaven for?"

FOR DISCUSSION AND REFLECTION

➤ Ask students to paraphrase Miles's explanation of Sisyphus's punishment. (Having students put the poem into their own words will allow you to check their understanding of Sisyphus's actions.)

➤ Why do you think Miles recasts Robert Browning's line to read "He said a man's reach must exceed his grasp, / Or what is Hades for?" (She turns the line on its head, suggesting that when man's reach exceeds his grasp, he is sure to be punished for it.)

➤ According to Josephine Miles, what is the belief that damned Sisyphus and the stone to everlasting torment? (It is believing that the process, not the goal, is what matters.)

W r i t i n g

QUICK ASSESS

Do students' notes:

✓ express the poem's point?

✓ provide specific quotations as support?

✓ judge the poem's effectiveness?

Students are asked to identify what, for them, is the point of the poem and then to determine how effective this poem is in achieving its purpose. Remind students that there is no one right answer. Have them share what they have written as the point of the poem before they go on to judge its effectiveness.

READING AND WRITING EXTENSIONS

➤ Albert Camus's *The Myth of Sisyphus* is a philosophical examination of contemporary nihilism and the need to confront absurdity as a condition of life. Have students read some of it and compare Camus's message with that of Josephine Miles.

➤ Ask students to write about a time when they felt that no matter how hard they tried to solve a problem or achieve a goal, they always seemed to fall down and find themselves back where they started. This might be a physical challenge or the challenge of a relationship.

Two Applying the Criteria

C r i t i c a l   R e a d i n g

FOCUS

Robert Calasso on myths:

"For centuries people have spoken of the Greek myths as of something to be rediscovered, reawoken. The truth is it is the myths that are still out there waiting to wake us and be seen by us, like a tree waiting to greet our newly opened eyes."

BACKGROUND

Louise Glück teaches poetry and creative writing at Williams College. In 1993 she received the Pulitzer Prize for her book *The Wild Iris*. Shifting between the mythic and the modern, her poetry teaches us to look at old, familiar stories in new ways. In "The Mountain," she uses a classroom moment and the myth of Sisyphus to reflect upon the life of an artist. As many teachers do, the speaker finds herself revising the lesson with her mouth open, replacing the message she had planned to deliver to her students about the joys of hard work and effort without hope of reward for the more honest admission that the artist is "obsessed with attainment" and lives in pursuit of "that place where he will live forever." She admits that the life of pushing "a rock up a mountain, knowing nothing / would come of this effort" is hell.

FOR DISCUSSION AND REFLECTION

➤ What do you think Glück means when the speaker says that "the life of art is a life of endless labor"? (Many assume that the life of the artist is one of utter freedom: free expression, free thinking, free love. This teacher wants to disabuse her students of such a misconception and so compares the work of an artist with the labor of Sisyphus.)

➤ Why does she say "I am secretly pushing a rock myself"? (The speaker knows that a teacher's words largely fall on deaf ears. Most likely these students, like those of Louise Glück, are there to learn from her how to be artists. They want more than a life of endless labor with no reward. Artists want to reach the mountain top.)

➤ Explain what you think Glück's final line means, "And the rock has added / height to the mountain." (The product of the artist's labor, the "burden" he or she has carried, will transform the world. This, according to Glück, is every artist's dream.)

W r i t i n g

QUICK ASSESS
Do students' notes:

✓ express the poem's point?

✓ show their judgment of the effectiveness of the poem?

Students are asked to answer the same three questions about "The Mountain" that they answered in Lesson One about "Sisyphus." Before they begin to write, review together what it means for a poem to be "effective."

READING AND WRITING EXTENSIONS

➤ Read to students Louise Glück's poem "Circe's Power" and encourage them to compare how she has used this mythical figure to present readers with a contemporary message: "I never turned anyone into a pig. / Some people are pigs; I make them / look like pigs."

➤ Ask students to write "A Day in the Life of a Poet." Have students explore what they think poets do all day and share their reflections with the class.

Three Comparing Two Poems

Critical Reading

FOCUS

Juxtaposing one poem with another forces readers to hone their analytical thinking skills.

BACKGROUND

In *Literature, The Evolving Canon*, Sven Birkerts explains that in order to write about poetry with any comprehension you need to know how to read poetry: "This reading will differ from other kinds — from reading the newspaper or a mystery novel, say — because poetry uses language at a much greater degree of concentration. You need to grasp the poem on many different levels, paying attention to the way that images and figures of speech enrich the meaning. You also need to think of meaning in a different way. It is not always a message that can be summarized."

➤ Remind students that before writing interpretively about poetry, they should read the poem not once but several times, read slowly and carefully with an ear for the language, pay close attention to line breaks and stanza breaks, determine the poet's tone and attitude, and research any unfamiliar words or references.

FOR DISCUSSION AND REFLECTION

➤ How does the ease with which you read a poem influence your judgment of the poem? (Most readers prefer poems that they understand without too much of a struggle. This is a good reason for becoming more adept at reading poetry; more poems will open up for you.)

➤ Discuss the rhythm, imagery, and diction in both poems about Sisyphus.

➤ In "Sisyphus," Josephine Miles begins with the myth. In "The Mountain," Louise Glück begins with herself in the classroom. How does this make a difference? (Miles reinterprets the myth for modern man. Glück uses it to explain a point—first to her students and then to herself.)

Writing

QUICK ASSESS

Do students' responses:

✓ make a judgment about which poem has used the myth more effectively?

✓ offer specific quotations as support?

Students are asked to make a judgment about whether "Sisyphus" by Josephine Miles or "The Mountain" by Louise Glück more effectively uses the Sisyphus myth to convey a point. Assure students that there is no right or wrong answer here, only more and less convincing interpretations. If students want to quote a short passage from the poem without setting the lines off from the text, they may do so by using quotation marks and a slash to indicate the line division.

READING AND WRITING EXTENSIONS

➤ Have students write an essay comparing two other poems they like. For organizational purposes, have students begin their essay by setting out the general basis of the comparison. They should then analyze one text in depth before taking up the other.

➤ Invite students to bring in to class their favorite love poem. Then, as a class, determine what criteria should be used for judging these poems in terms of their effectiveness in conveying the experience of love.

Four Sentiment and Sentimentality

Critical Reading

FOCUS
Sentimentality is indulgence in emotion for its own sake, or expression of more emotion than an occasion warrants.

BACKGROUND

Sentiment is a refined feeling, a keen or delicate sensibility expressed in a work of art. It can be a challenge when working with students to distinguish between sentiment and sentimentality because they often find an adult's attitude toward sentimental art or poetry elitist and a rejection of their own honest response to a work. It is important to tread carefully and not demean their emerging sensibilities. One way to do this is to bring in greeting cards that are full of gushing and trite expressions and use these as your touchstone for sentimental verse. John Updike's poem describes the death of a puppy, a subject that in the hands of a lesser poet would inevitably fall into the realm of sentimentality.

➤ Over the past three decades, John Updike has emerged as one of our most prolific and versatile men of letters, writing essays, stories, novels, art criticism, and speeches. His fiction holds up a mirror to our changing society, exploring the manners and morals of the upper-middle class.

FOR DISCUSSION AND REFLECTION

➤ What is it about the death of a puppy that might easily lead a writer to treat the subject in a sentimental manner? (The sweet innocence of a puppy engages most readers immediately. Her suffering tugs at anyone's heartstrings.)

➤ How well does John Updike avoid this pitfall? (Answers will vary, but Updike avoids clichés and abstractions in favor of concrete images and events. Instead of writing about the generalized death of a puppy, he has given readers a specific account of his own family pet. We see "the children were noisily fed" and hear his wife's voice "imperious with tears.")

➤ Explain how the last stanza brings the poem full circle. (After the puppy has died, the couple return home to find that even in pain she had tried to earn their praise. She was a "good dog.")

Writing

QUICK ASSESS

Do students' responses:

✓ offer a clear opinion about whether the poem is sentimental?

✓ support their opinion on "Dog's Death" with appropriate evidence?

Students are asked to write their opinion about whether "Dog's Death" is a sentimental poem. Encourage them to cite specific lines and phrases from the poem as evidence for their point of view.

READING AND WRITING EXTENSIONS

➤ Have the class pretend that tomorrow is St. Valentine's Day and ask students to write two imaginary love letters to themselves—one from a sentimental person and one from a person who feels deeply about them but who possesses a certain amount of emotional reserve, a command over his or her feelings.

➤ One of John Updike's best poems is "Ex-Basketball Player." Read this piece to students and again discuss how he avoids a sentimental treatment of his subject through his careful use of language.

Five Precise Diction

Critical Reading

FOCUS

Diction refers to an author's word choice and the level of language.

BACKGROUND

Diction is a writer's choice of individual words, the vocabulary chosen for a particular poem or story. Diction can be formal or informal, technical or common, abstract or concrete. In "The Great Blue Heron," Carolyn Kizer uses diction that is precise to describe a day from her childhood when she spotted a strange bird along the beach. The heron's humpbacked stance caused her to wonder, "'Heron, whose ghost are you?'" Without quite understanding why, she ran to find her mother, but by the time the two returned to the shore, "The spectral bird was gone." Fifteen years later, the narrator recalls that afternoon and once again addresses the heron to ask, "Why have you followed me here, / Heavy and far away?" In the final eight lines of the poem she answers her own question as she comes to understand that it was "Waiting upon the day / When, like gray smoke, a vapor / floating into the sky, / A handful of paper ashes, / My mother would drift away."

➤ Given that the heron is such a central image in this poem, students who are unfamiliar with the bird may find a picture helpful to their understanding of Kizer's poem. One can be easily found in an encyclopedia or on the Internet.

FOR DISCUSSION AND REFLECTION

➤ Ask students to describe in their own words the opening scene of this poem. (A child on the beach alone sights a heron and wonders about its strange presence in a summer day.)

➤ Why do you think the child runs to her mother? (On a first reading, students may simply see this as the natural response of any child to show his or her mother what she has found. With rereading, they may find that the "sudden chill" this child felt was a premonition of the day when her mother would no longer be there for her to run to.)

➤ What connotations does the phrase "spectral bird" conjure up for you? (Many responses are possible. Ghostly, "spectral" images are often associated with death and dying.)

Writing

QUICK ASSESS

Do students' judgments:

✓ clearly evaluate the poem's language?

✓ rest on carefully established criteria?

✓ include specific text references as support?

After paraphrasing part of the poem, students are asked to evaluate Carolyn Kizer's poem "The Great Blue Heron" in terms of its use of language. Begin by brainstorming together the criteria one might use when judging a poem in this manner.

READING AND WRITING EXTENSIONS

➤ Have students write about an incident from their childhood when they remember having called a parent over to see what they had seen or done. They may choose to write this memory as a story, poem, or short play.

➤ Read Carolyn Kizer's "Thrall" from her collection *Mermaids in the Basement*. Ask students to discuss the differences in the way Kizer writes about her mother in "The Great Blue Heron" and her father in "Thrall."

U n i t   O v e r v i e w

In this unit, students are invited to take an in-depth look at the writings of Truman Capote. As they read one of his short stories, a description of a person, and the comments of a literary critic about his style, students will explore the use of local color details, the dualities in Capote's works, his depiction of character weaknesses, and his gothic mixtures of fantasy and reality.

L i t e r a t u r e   F o c u s

	Lesson	Literature
1.	Local Color	**"Louis Armstrong"** from *Observations* (Nonfiction)
2.	Dualities	**"Miriam"** (Short Story)
3.	Subtle Description	**"Miriam"** (Short Story)
4.	Gothic Style	**"Miriam"** (Short Story)
5.	Reading Literary Criticism	**James Dickey,** from a speech (Nonfiction)

R e a d i n g   F o c u s

1. Writers enhance their writing with carefully chosen details that place the reader in a specific time and place.
2. Contrast is one of the strongest ways to describe characters in literature.
3. Writers can develop plots through subtle indications of the strengths and weaknesses of a character.
4. Readers must form and support their interpretations of a story after carefully considering the details.
5. Literary critics can sometimes help readers see new aspects of an author's work.

W r i t i n g   F o c u s

1. Write a sketch of a person, including local color details.
2. Examine the contrast between two characters in a short story.
3. Analyze a character's weaknesses.
4. In a letter to a friend, interpret a character's behavior and personality.
5. Analyze and respond to what a literary critic has said about Truman Capote's writing.

One Local Color

Critical Reading

FOCUS

Truman Capote, a master of local color, from in *Other Voices, Other Rooms*:

"He leaped off the stump, and made for the house, his loosened shirt-tail flying behind; run, run, run, his heart told him, and wham! he'd pitched headlong into a briar patch."

BACKGROUND

Truman Capote was an American novelist, short story writer, and playwright whose early writing extended and adapted the Southern gothic tradition. He later developed a more journalistic approach, beginning with *Observations* (1959), from which this selection on Louis Armstrong is taken. Capote's most famous work, *In Cold Blood* (1966), is an account of a multiple murder committed by two sociopaths. He called what he had written a nonfiction novel. Capote said of himself, "I started writing when I was eight—out of the blue, uninspired by any example. I'd never known anyone who wrote; in fact, I knew few people who read. But the fact was, the only four things that interested me were: reading books, going to the movies, tap dancing, and drawing pictures."

➤ Describing himself as a young writer, Capote said, "The most interesting writing I did during those days were the plain everyday observations that I recorded in my journal. Long verbatim accounts of overheard conversations. Local gossip. A kind of reporting, a style of seeing and hearing that would later seriously influence me."

FOR DISCUSSION AND REFLECTION

➤ From the details available in this passage, what kind of child do you think Truman Capote was? (Answers will vary, but at least he seemed to love the spotlight and attention.)

➤ Bring in a recording of Louis Armstrong's music and ask students how the real thing compares with what they imagined this music might sound like based upon Capote's description.

➤ Do you find it credible that Truman Capote can remember this vividly events that occurred when he was only four? (Many points of view are possible. Great writers often possess this uncanny ability to recall and recreate the past.)

Writing

QUICK ASSESS

Do students' sketches:

✓ include details of local color?

✓ establish time and place?

✓ use specific, evocative words and details?

Students are asked to write a brief sketch of a person they know well. Have them consider what local color details they would want to be sure to include in order to establish time and place.

READING AND WRITING EXTENSIONS

➤ Have students write a brief sketch of an animal they know well. This could be a family pet or a bird that has taken a liking to their balcony. Have them be sure to include local color details in their description.

➤ Ask students to look up Louis Armstrong in a biographical encyclopedia in the library and compare this sketch of the man with the one by Capote.

Two Dualities

Critical Reading

FOCUS
Truman Capote's work often contains contrasts—in themes, settings, and characters.

BACKGROUND
In *Writers at Work*, Truman Capote explained that "I invariably have the illusion that the whole play of a story, its start and middle and finish, occur in my mind simultaneously—that I'm seeing it in one flash. At one time I used to keep little notebooks with outlines for stories. But I found doing this somehow deadened the idea in my imagination. If the notion is good enough, if it truly belongs to you, then you can't forget it . . . it will haunt you till it's written."

➤ In his short story "Miriam," Truman Capote created a haunting tale of a lonely widow who finds herself possessed of a strange new friend.

FOR DISCUSSION AND REFLECTION
➤ Based upon these first pages of the story, what can you tell about Mrs. Miller? (She lives alone, has no friends, sticks close to home, leads an ordered life with few vices and fewer pleasures.)

➤ What is strange and unsettling about the appearance of Miriam? (She has waist-length, silver-white hair, wears expensive clothing, speaks like an adult, is oddly assertive, and acts spontaneously.)

➤ What would you do if someone like Miriam approached you in this way? (Help students to see that how they respond says much about themselves.)

Writing

QUICK ASSESS
Do students' writings:

✓ focus on one significant characteristic?

✓ analyze the significance of the contrast?

Students are asked to select one characteristic of either Miriam or Mrs. Miller and then explain what the contrast reveals. If Mrs. Miller cares little for her appearance, why is it significant that Miriam's outfit is so precise and even lavish? Draw students' attention to the way these two characters seem to represent two sides of one person.

READING AND WRITING EXTENSIONS
➤ Have students write a description of an unusual-looking stranger. Encourage them to include descriptive details that establish the setting and local color.

➤ Read students the first pages of Robert Louis Stevenson's *Dr. Jekyll and Mr. Hyde*: "Mr. Utterson the lawyer was a man of a rugged countenance, that was never lighted by a smile; cold, scanty and embarrassed in discourse; backward in sentiment; lean, long, dusty, dreary, and yet somehow lovable. He was austere with himself; drank gin when he was alone, to mortify a taste for vintages; and though he enjoyed the theater, had not crossed the doors of one for twenty years." Have students compare Stevenson's tone with that of Capote.

Three Subtle Description

Critical Reading

FOCUS

Writers bring their characters to life through dialogue, setting, and action.

BACKGROUND

In an interview in the November 1967 issue of *McCall's*, Truman Capote said, "Writing was always an obsession with me, quite simply something I had to do, and I don't understand exactly why this should have been true. It was as if I were an oyster and somebody forced a grain of sand into my shell — a grain of sand that I didn't know was there and didn't particularly welcome. Then a pearl started forming around the grain and it irritated me, made me angry, tortured me sometimes. But the oyster can't help becoming obsessed with the pearl."

FOR DISCUSSION AND REFLECTION

➤ What does Miriam's persistence at the door suggest about her character? (She is not hampered by the usual conventions of behavior. She does what she likes regardless of how this might inconvenience or disturb Mrs. Miller. She seems oblivious to anyone's feelings but her own.)

➤ What does Mrs. Miller's reaction to Miriam's sudden reappearance at her doorstep reveal about her character? (She allows herself to be pushed around by the little girl. She allows herself to be distracted from important questions such as how Miriam knew where she lived. She is kind and feeds the hungry child. She expects promises to be kept.)

➤ What does Miriam's hunger suggest? (Answers may include that this is a ravenous character who will not be satisfied until she has devoured/destroyed Mrs. Miller.)

Writing

QUICK ASSESS

Do students' responses:

✓ identify moments when Miriam gains power?

✓ explain the weakness in Mrs. Miller that allows this to happen?

Students are asked to explain the character weakness that allows Miriam to gain power over Mrs. Miller. It may help students to reread the opening paragraph of the story, in which Mrs. Miller is first described, to see how the seeds of this weakness are sown early in the reader's mind.

READING AND WRITING EXTENSIONS

➤ Have students read Truman Capote's widely anthologized "A Christmas Memory" and compare his character description there with that in "Miriam." For example, have them consider this sentence: "A woman with shorn white hair is standing at the kitchen window. She is wearing tennis shoes and a shapeless gray sweater over a summery calico dress. She is small and sprightly, like a bantam hen; but due to a long youthful illness, her shoulders are pitifully hunched."

➤ Ask students to write about a time when someone gained power over them and then used that power to their disadvantage. Have them think about what aspect of their own character made them vulnerable to this person.

Four Gothic Style

Critical Reading

FOCUS
Gothic style is characterized by grotesque, macabre, or fantastic incidents or by an atmosphere of irrational violence, desolation, and decay.

BACKGROUND
Edgar Allan Poe was tormented throughout his life by painful loss, bitterness, and depression. He found escape in writing stories and poems that portrayed haunted lives even darker than his own. Truman Capote's gothic style, like Poe's, explores the dark side of the mind and the heart. The pages in Lesson Four describe Miriam's final invasion of Mrs. Miller. Just when the woman thinks she is safe and able once again to be "the person who lived in this room, who cooked her own meals, who owned a canary, who was someone she could trust and believe in: Mrs. H. T. Miller," the specter reappears: "'Hello,' said Miriam."

FOR DISCUSSION AND REFLECTION
➤ How well did your predictions match the ending to this story? (Have students explain why they thought as they did about how "Miriam" might end.)

➤ What purpose do the neighbors serve in the narrative? (They represent the practical, real world. They respond to Mrs. Miller's call for help with simple, forthright advice, "What you shoulda done, you shoulda called a cop.")

➤ What in the ending contributes to the gothic style of the story? (The empty room, the growing darkness, and the eerie sound all help to create the gothic setting. Plus, for a moment, the reader is persuaded that Mrs. Miller has recovered from this nightmare and can now go back to being her normal self. In the final paragraphs, she hears sounds from the next room of drawers being opened and closed. Miriam is moving in.)

Writing

QUICK ASSESS
Do students' letters:
✓ explain Mrs. Miller's behavior and personality?
✓ use appropriate quotations from the story as support?

Students are asked to write a letter to a friend interpreting Mrs. Miller's behavior and personality. Before they begin to write, brainstorm on the board possible interpretations of what has occurred in this short story. Remind them that either interpretation of Miriam—as real or as a hallucination—is valid as long as they support it with evidence from the text.

READING AND WRITING EXTENSIONS
➤ Read Edgar Allan Poe's famous narrative poem "The Raven." Ask students to consider how this story of a man grieving over the loss of his beloved, the beautiful Lenore, is similar in tone to "Miriam."

➤ Based upon what they know about Mrs. Miller, have students describe what they think Mr. Miller must have been like. Remind the class that the only information Capote has given about the man is that "Mr. H. T. Miller had left a reasonable amount of insurance."

Five Reading Literary Criticism

Critical Reading

FOCUS

Truman Capote's personal vision "runs to unforgettable images of fear, hopelessness, and dream-death."

BACKGROUND

In the preface to *Music for Chameleons*, Truman Capote wrote, "The problem was: how can a writer successfully combine within a single form—say the short story—all he knows about every other form of writing? For this was why my work was often insufficiently illuminated; the voltage was there, but by restricting myself to the techniques of whatever form I was working in, I was not using everything I knew about writing— all I'd learned from film scripts, plays, reportage, poetry, the short story, novellas, the novel. A writer ought to have all his colors, all his abilities available on the same palette for mingling."

➤ In the speech in this lesson, delivered at the annual meeting of the American Academy and Institute of Arts and Letters, James Dickey paints a rich picture of Capote's prose.

FOR DISCUSSION AND REFLECTION

➤ What comments of Dickey's regarding Capote's writing particularly struck you for their accuracy? (Encourage students to connect quotes from Dickey's speech with examples from "Miriam" or "Louis Armstrong.")

➤ Why do you think James Dickey rereads Truman Capote's work? What in a book causes you to return again and again to the same text? (Many responses are possible. Offer students examples of authors whose work continues to bring you pleasure.)

➤ Dickey refers to Capote's "craft as an artist." How would you define this? (Students will offer a range of answers, including an engaging style, a unique voice, the ability to plot a story well, well-crafted characters, and the effective use of language.)

Writing

QUICK ASSESS

Do students' analyses:

✓ reflect understanding of Dickey's points?

✓ clearly agree or disagree with Dickey's comments?

✓ cite specific textual references?

Students are asked to write an analysis of the points Dickey makes about Capote's work, agreeing or disagreeing with the critic. Remind students that literary critics are first and foremost readers. To be sure, they have a great deal of experience, and the best of them care a great deal about literature, but critics do not have a secret formula for determining a work's meanings or purposes. Just like us, they read and think.

READING AND WRITING EXTENSIONS

➤ Have students read another Truman Capote story from *A Tree of Night* and compare their response with that of James Dickey. Do they find in this story the "lenslike detachment" that Dickey praises?

➤ Ask students to write a letter to the English Department chairman at their school in which they recommend that the work of Truman Capote should continue to be included in the 11th grade curriculum or that it should be deleted from the list of readings.

U n i t   O v e r v i e w

In "Essentials of Reading," students explore five strategies that active readers use: making predictions, analyzing tone, reading between the lines, thinking about theme, and examining an author's purpose. They will practice these strategies as they read and discuss short stories by Jerome Weidman and Ernest Hemingway, an excerpt of Charles Frazier's novel *Cold Mountain*, and a passage from James Baldwin's memoir, *Notes of a Native Son*.

L i t e r a t u r e   F o c u s

	Lesson	Literature
1.	Thinking With the Writer	**Jerome Weidman,** "My Father Sits in the Dark" (Short Story)
2.	Analyzing Tone	**Charles Frazier,** from *Cold Mountain* (Novel)
3.	Reading Between the Lines	**Ernest Hemingway,** "The End of Something" (Short Story)
4.	Thinking Theme	
5.	Author's Purpose	**James Baldwin,** from *Notes of a Native Son* (Nonfiction)

R e a d i n g   F o c u s

1. Active readers know that making predictions as they read will help them focus on the essential details and information.

2. Tone is the overall feeling, or effect, created by a writer's use of words, imagery, and rhythm.

3. Critical readers know that making inferences about a story's characters will improve their understanding of the work as a whole.

4. If you can understand the story's theme, you can identify and understand the message the author has for you.

5. An important first step in understanding the author's intent is understanding the tone of the writing.

W r i t i n g   F o c u s

1. Write a letter in which a character explains his feelings to a friend.
2. Compare the tone of two poems.
3. Compose a letter of advice that a character might receive.
4. Identify a story's themes.
5. Examine an author's purpose and tone.

One Thinking With the Writer

Critical Reading

FOCUS

An active reader makes predictions about what will happen next.

BACKGROUND

In "My Father Sits in the Dark," the narrator puzzles over his father's habit of sitting up late into the night alone. This is an ideal story for teaching students about making predictions because the narrator himself is doing the same: "Why doesn't he tell me? I have a funny feeling that until I get an answer, I will go crazy." Just before the first place where students are asked to stop and predict why they think the father sits in the kitchen in the dark, the narrator asks himself, "How could it be restful to sit alone in an uncomfortable chair far into the night, in darkness? What can it be?" Later in the story, the son confronts his father with his question, "Why don't you go to bed? Why do you sit here so late in the dark?" The story itself invites readers to ask themselves questions about what is likely to happen next.

FOR DISCUSSION AND REFLECTION

➤ What similarities, if any, did you notice between the father and son? (It is interesting to note that both father and son are awake late into the night and that both seem to be creatures of habit—for example, the father's smoking and the son's water drinking.)

➤ What do you think most bothers the son about his father's habit of sitting in the dark? (Many responses are possible. It worries the son that something may be bothering his father that the older man is unable to talk about or share. It is also an aspect of his father that the son wants to understand.)

➤ How well did your final prediction about the father's answer match with the story's ending? (Students are likely to predict much more dramatic answers than the one the father provides.)

Writing

QUICK ASSESS

Do students' letters:

✓ describe the son's worries?

✓ reveal the father's thoughts?

Students are asked to write a letter from the father to a friend explaining his own preference for thinking in the dark and why he has difficulty making his son understand his reasons for doing so. As a prewriting activity, have one student pretend to be the father and have the rest of the class pose questions to him about his nocturnal habits. When this student runs out of answers, have another take his or her place.

READING AND WRITING EXTENSIONS

➤ Have students write about a time they have felt puzzled by one of their parents' behavior or seeming preoccupation.

➤ Ask students to read Theodore Roethke's poem "My Papa's Waltz" and compare this boy's response to his father's behavior with the attitude of the narrator in "My Father Sits in the Dark."

Two Analyzing Tone

Critical Reading

FOCUS
Charles Frazier's novel *Cold Mountain* provides a window for a reader that opens "onto some other place and lets him walk through and be there."

BACKGROUND
Set near the end of the Civil War, *Cold Mountain* is the story of a wounded Confederate veteran, Inman, who gets up from his hospital bed and begins the journey back to his home and to the woman he loves. In these opening paragraphs of the novel, Charles Frazier sets the tone for the rest of his story. By carefully examining his rhythm, word choice, and imagery, a reader can determine the properties of the voice and the telling style of the author or the author's chosen narrator. Tone is directly related to point of view. How the story is told depends on who is telling it and has everything to do with the narrator's relation to the events.

FOR DISCUSSION AND REFLECTION
➤ What can you tell about Inman from the first three paragraphs of the novel *Cold Mountain*? (Many responses are possible, including that he is seriously wounded, that he is a reader and a pensive and patient man, that he seems drawn to the world outside the hospital window, that he wants to escape from his recent memories of war.)

➤ Why do you think Frazier chose to set the opening scene of his book in the hazy dawn? (Just like Inman, the reader cannot quite see what is before him. There is a sense of what lies ahead but no clear shape yet.)

➤ What do you think the author is referring to in the passage, "for he had seen the metal face of the age and had been so stunned by it that when he thought into the future, all he could vision was a world from which everything he counted important had been banished or had willingly fled"? (The battlefield was antithetical to life as Inman knew it. He seems to want to leave it behind and return to the simpler world of his youth.)

Writing

QUICK ASSESS
Do students responses:
✓ compare the tone of the two pieces?
✓ explain how the tone affects readers' impressions of the characters?

Students are asked to compare the tone of this excerpt with that of "My Father Sits in the Dark." Before they begin to write, invite students to put examples on the board of words and phrases that helped them to determine the tone of each of the pieces.

READING AND WRITING EXTENSIONS
➤ Have students research Civil War hospitals and look for historical details about the treatment of wounded soldiers in the South, as a way to recreate the world where Inman stood in this opening scene.

➤ Ask students to read portions of Michael Shaara's *The Killer Angels*, a Pulitzer Prize-winning Civil War novel about the Battle of Gettysburg. Have them compare this realistic portrayal of war written in a factual tone with Frazier's more reflective tone.

Three Reading Between the Lines

C r i t i c a l   R e a d i n g

FOCUS

Ernest Hemingway on writing:

"In going where you have to go, and doing what you have to do, you dull and blunt the instrument you write with. But I would rather have it bent and dull and know I had to put it on the grindstone again and hammer it into shape, and know that I had something to write about, than to have it bright and shining and nothing to say, or smooth and well-oiled in the closet, but unused."

BACKGROUND

A cursory reading of a literary work will rarely produce a full understanding. After a first reading, it may be embarrassingly difficult to answer pointed questions or to say anything intelligent about the work. Readers first follow the story and attempt to piece together what is happening, but in order to understand the significance of these events, they must also make inferences about what is happening. In "The End of Something," Nick and Marjorie go fishing in Hortons Bay. Nothing obviously terrible occurs in the course of their day, but by the end of it the couple has split up. To figure out why, students will need to re-examine the story for details that suggest what has happened in this relationship.

FOR DISCUSSION AND REFLECTION

➤ What evidence can you find that suggests something is wrong with the relationship? (Students may point to Marjorie's romantic reference to the mill as "our old ruin." Nick replies, "There it is." Nick's negative response to the fish biting implies that he also has a negative attitude toward their relationship. "'They're feeding,' Marjorie said. 'But they won't strike,' Nick said." She is optimistic. He is pessimistic.)

➤ What can you infer from Nick's statement that Marjorie "knows everything"? (Many responses are possible, including Nick's insecurity and unwillingness to talk about how he feels other than commenting that "It isn't fun any more.")

➤ How would you respond if someone you cared about said that love with you wasn't fun any more? (After students respond, have them reread the passage describing what Marjorie and Nick do after he says this. Notice that he literally pushes her away.)

W r i t i n g

QUICK ASSESS

Do students' notes:

✓ offer advice to Marjorie?

✓ use comments from their inference charts?

Students are asked to imagine they are Marjorie's friend who gives her advice about what to do next about Nick. Have students share what they have written in their inference charts with one another before they begin to write their advice.

READING AND WRITING EXTENSIONS

➤ Have students read Hemingway's "The Short Happy Life of Francis Macomber" and compare the relationship between the couple in this story with that of Marjorie and Nick.

➤ Ask students to imagine they are Nick. Have them write a diary entry for the day described in this story.

Four Thinking Theme

Critical Reading

FOCUS

Theme is the statement about life an author is trying to get across in a work of literature.

BACKGROUND

Though theme is central to fiction, it can also be elusive. Young readers often feel that the theme of a work is something that only teachers can identify and that if they simply sit back and wait, we will simply tell them. Sven Birkerts explains that experienced readers know that "themes are often complex and shaded with ambiguity. In many cases they are woven deeply into the fabric of the work and cannot be plucked free with a single motion. This embeddedness may prove to be an obstacle to the reader who would grab the message and move on, but in fact it is part of what makes the reading of fiction worthwhile. As readers concerned with theme, we need to cultivate both patience and a taste for ambiguities and shades of meaning."

FOR DISCUSSION AND REFLECTION

➤ What do the things Hemingway spends the most time describing in the story tell us about his purposes for telling the story? (Students may point to the story's dialogue as strong evidence of a relationship where two people are not communicating well.)

➤ What does Bill's question toward the end of the story, "Did she go all right?" suggest to you about Nick's attitude toward Marjorie? (Many responses are possible but should lead to the suggestion that Nick planned to break off his relationship with her on this fishing trip.)

➤ What does the next line, "'Oh, yes,' Nick said, lying, his face on the blanket," tell you about how breaking up with Marjorie really went for Nick? (He is not as nonchalant about it as he would pretend to his friend. Maybe some of his callousness is feigned.)

Writing

QUICK ASSESS

Do students' responses:

✓ identify themes in "The End of Something"?

✓ reflect a careful reading of the story?

Students are asked to identify the themes in "The End of Something." Begin by having them share with a partner what they have written about Hemingway's attitude in the story. Discuss together how a writer's attitude towards his subject is an important clue to the work's themes.

READING AND WRITING EXTENSIONS

➤ Have students take one of the themes they have identified in "The End of Something" and write a story of their own that explores this subject. Suggest they use different characters and another set of events.

➤ Ask students to read "A Clean, Well-Lighted Place" by Ernest Hemingway and share with the class the various themes that he seems to be exploring in this work.

Five Author's Purpose

Critical Reading

FOCUS

All of James Baldwin's writings bear some stamp of his assertion that "all art is a kind of confession."

BACKGROUND

Unlike an autobiography, a memoir focuses upon the author's response to people and events. A memoir is often anecdotal or intimate in tone. Some writers of memoir have played roles in, or have been close observers of, historical events, and their main purpose is to describe or interpret those events. Living as he did during the civil rights movement in the United States, James Baldwin describes people and events in his own life with an eye toward illuminating the subject of race in America. Baldwin grew up in poverty in Harlem.

FOR DISCUSSION AND REFLECTION

➤ How does the inclusion of "I think" in the first sentence influence your reading of the character sketch? (It tells the reader immediately that this is a work in progress, that the writing is a means for the author of coming to understand his father.)

➤ What do you think Baldwin means when he says that his father "knew that he was black but did not know that he was beautiful"? (Students should see that the son, James Baldwin, recognized the beauty in his father's blackness that the father's experience of racism did not allow him to see in himself.)

➤ Why do you think that this man's children were never "glad to see him come home"? (Many responses are possible. Evidence in the passage suggests that Baldwin's father was a man who cared deeply about his children, but his only means of demonstrating his concern were "outrageously demanding and protective." Also, he "almost unfailingly" brought home the wrong surprise. The children were terrified of his wrath.)

Writing

QUICK ASSESS

Do students' responses:

✔ describe the tone Baldwin employs in this piece?

✔ identify Baldwin's purpose?

✔ connect the tone to the author's intent?

Students are asked to describe Baldwin's purpose in this piece about his father. In order to help students visualize Baldwin's father, draw the outline of a head on the board and have students contribute physical and emotional details that make up this man's character.

READING AND WRITING EXTENSIONS

➤ James Baldwin was one of the foremost essayists of his time. Have students read "Many Thousands Gone," which begins with this passage: "It is only in his music, which Americans are able to admire because a protective sentimentality limits their understanding of it, that the Negro in America has been able to tell his story. It is a story which otherwise has yet to be told and which no American is prepared to hear."

➤ Invite students to write a character sketch of their own mother or father, using words and images that create a tone and suggest their attitude toward this important person in their life.

HISTORY THROUGH STORY

Unit Overview

In this unit, students explore stories based on historical events, specifically the internment of Japanese Americans during World War II. As they read a personal narrative, a twice-told story, a poem, a vignette, and an excerpt from a novel, they learn about the ways in which writers can share the personal and public meaning of important events.

Literature Focus

	Lesson	Literature
1.	Personal Narratives	**Yoshiko Uchida,** from *The Invisible Thread* (Autobiography)
2.	A Twice-Told Story	**Jeanne Wakatsuki Houston,** from *Farewell to Manzanar* (Novel)
3.	Responding Through a Poem	**Dwight Okita,** "In Response to Executive Order 9066" (Poetry)
4.	Vignette as Commentary	**John Sunford,** "Shikata Ga Nai" from *The Winters of That Country* (Nonfiction)
5.	Fictionalizing History	**David Guterson,** from *Snow Falling on Cedars* (Novel)

Reading Focus

1. Personal narratives are retellings of real events that carefully reconstruct the personal experience to reveal the author's reactions to them and their significance.
2. Often writers present the past and present simultaneously in a personal narrative. It allows them to review the events of the past from a more objective perspective.
3. Many poems retell incidents concisely, focusing on key details and using tone to great effect.
4. Vignettes are short episodes or scenes that rely on visual imagery and description. They create a picture in the reader's mind and provide indirect commentary from the writer.
5. Writers who fictionalize historical events often use omniscient narrators and stream of consciousness to emphasize or dramatize the aspects of the real situation that they can imagine but cannot actually know.

Writing Focus

1. Write a personal narrative.
2. Rewrite a narrative, describing past events as well as present action.
3. Write a poem about a personal experience.
4. Sketch a scene.
5. Dramatize an incident using an omniscient narrator and stream of consciousness.

One Personal Narratives

Critical Reading

FOCUS

In her autobiography, Yoshiko Uchida explains that "I was still a prisoner, simply because I had not been able to evacuate voluntarily. It didn't make sense."

BACKGROUND

In this excerpt from her autobiography *The Invisible Thread*, Yoshiko Uchida tells the story of her family's relocation from a camp in California to another camp in Utah. She describes the train journey as a novelist might, portraying details from the landscape as well as her own actions in ways that elicit a strong response from readers. While an autobiography is technically nonfiction, it is important for students to see how the genre cannot help but be a subjective treatment of the historical moment it describes; Uchida is hardly a disinterested narrator of these events.

FOR DISCUSSION AND REFLECTION

➤ What evidence can you find in this excerpt that supports Uchida's description of herself as a "prisoner"? (A row of Military Policemen stand between the train and the desert when they halt. The passengers are "counted again" as they get off.)

➤ How does knowing that Yoshiko Uchida was five months from graduating from the University of California in Berkeley influence your view of her as a narrator? (Her maturity and education suggest that she is a reliable narrator. Though her emotional response to events may color her reporting, she is no bewildered child.)

➤ Uchida refers to the place as a "concentration camp," a term more commonly used to describe the Nazi death camps of Auschwitz, Treblinka, and Bergen-Belsen. In what ways did the Japanese relocation camps resemble the camps in Europe? (Answers will depend upon students' familiarity with the camps, but should include the illegal detainment of a specific group of people.)

Writing

QUICK ASSESS

Do students' narratives:

✓ focus on a difficult situation?

✓ include details of the setting?

✓ reveal their feelings about the incident?

Students are asked to write a personal narrative that describes a time when they felt they were in a difficult position or felt like an outsider. As students will be reworking this same incident throughout this cluster of lessons, take time to brainstorm many possible incidents from which they might choose their narrative.

READING AND WRITING EXTENSIONS

➤ Read to students Gretel Ehrlich's novel *Heart Mountain* (pages 28-34) in which another train ride to a relocation camp is described, this time in Wyoming: "The train's whistle blew long and hard and Kai heard the crossing bells where a county road intersected the tracks. There was nothing to see but grainfields, unfenced grazing land, and a tiny town in the distance shrouded by cottonwood trees."

➤ Ask students to imagine that they are Uchida's friend Helen. Have them write her diary entry for the day described in this excerpt.

Two A Twice-Told Story

Critical Reading

FOCUS
Jeanne Wakatsuki Houston on writing a twice-told story:

"Writing it has been a way of coming to terms with the impact these years have had on my entire life."

BACKGROUND
Jeanne Wakatsuki Houston explains how she and her husband set out to write about the life inside Manzanar, where her family spent three and a half years: "We began with a tape recorder and an old 1944 yearbook put together at Manzanar High School. It documented the entire camp scene—the graduating seniors, the guard towers, the Judo pavilion, the creeks I used to wade in, my family's barracks. As the photos brought that world back, I began to dredge up feelings that had lain submerged since the forties. I began to make connections I had previously been afraid to see. It had taken me twenty-five years to reach the point where I could talk openly about Manzanar, and the more I talked, the clearer it became that any book we wrote would have to include a good deal more than day-to-day life inside the compound. To tell what I knew and felt about it would mean telling something about our family before the war, and the years that followed the war, and about my father's past, as well as my own way of seeing things now. Writing it has been a way of coming to terms with the impact these years have had on my entire life."

➤ Read and then discuss Henry Steele Commager's statement in *Harper's Magazine* in 1947: "It is sobering to recall that though the Japanese relocation program, carried through at such incalculable cost in misery and tragedy, was justified on the ground that the Japanese were potentially disloyal, the record does not disclose a single case of Japanese disloyalty or sabotage during the whole war."

FOR DISCUSSION AND REFLECTION
➤ Why do you think Jeanne Wakatsuki Houston wanted her own children to visit Manzanar? (Students will likely speculate that she wants them to understand the experiences that have shaped her life and, as a result, their own.)

➤ What do you think the author suggests when she writes that "Even the dust is gone"? (All trace of the years she and so many others spent in this internment camp has vanished. Many would like to forget that Manzanar ever existed.)

➤ Why do you think Houston hears voices as she walks near the Japanese memorial? (She is sensitive to the ghosts of those who lived and died in Manzanar. She uses her writer's voice to allow theirs to be heard.)

Writing

QUICK ASSESS
Do students' stories:

✔ review the past incident?

✔ describe present action?

Students are asked to rewrite their story from Lesson One as a twice-told tale. Allow students who no longer see potential in their first choice of incident to choose another from their list of possible subjects.

READING AND WRITING EXTENSIONS
➤ Have students write about a time when their parents wanted them to visit somewhere or someone that they had little interest in seeing.

➤ Read all of *Farewell to Manzanar* and discuss how the author uses a storyteller's techniques to teach readers about historical events.

Three Responding Through a Poem

Critical Reading

FOCUS

A poet's concise treatment of an historical event may be powerfully dramatic.

BACKGROUND

Executive Order 9066 required Japanese Americans to report to internment camps. Though the order was reversed in 1944 and Japanese Americans were awarded damages from the government for their suffering, the pain of these days remained in the hearts of thousands of individuals. Dwight Okita's mother was one of them. In this poem, Okita takes on his mother's voice and attempts to recreate the way in which she would have bid her best friend good-bye before being sent to an internment camp. The subtext of the poem is the personal cost of such an executive order on innocent children who have no idea why their lives have been disrupted. Its genius resides in its ability to avoid sentimentality. Okita has also written a play, *Letters I Never Wrote,* as a spin-off from this poem.

FOR DISCUSSION AND REFLECTION

➤ Why do you think the speaker in this poem makes reference to chopsticks and hot dogs? (Answers will likely include a discussion of how the girl is more comfortable with American food than Japanese food and, by association, identifies more closely with American culture than with Japanese culture.)

➤ How would you describe Okita's tone in this poem? (The opening lines suggest that his tone is ironic. The letter begins with a formal acceptance of an invitation. In fact, the girl has no choice but to go where she has been directed.)

➤ Why do you think the girl's friend, Denise O'Connor, responds as she does? (Many responses are possible, but they should focus on attitudes towards "the Enemy" in wartime. The friendship has been sacrificed to patriotism.)

➤ What do you think is the significance of the girl's gift of tomato seeds? (She seems to recognize that there is no way to answer Denise's accusation. Her only hope is that in the time it will take for these seeds to germinate, memories of their friendship will resurface and replace the hateful feelings Denise has harbored for her.)

Writing

QUICK ASSESS

Do students' poems:

✓ retell the story effectively?

✓ use imagery?

Students are asked to rewrite some aspect of their own incident as a poem. Using Dwight Okita's example of narrowing his subject to two characters may help students compress their stories.

READING AND WRITING EXTENSIONS

➤ For another view of internment camps, have students read from *Empire of the Sun,* J. G. Ballard's boyhood memoir of his experiences in a Japanese internment camp for British citizens during World War II.

➤ Ask students to write a letter from Denise to Dwight Okita's mother in the internment camp after the first tomato has ripened.

Four Vignette as Commentary

Critical Reading

FOCUS

In a vignette describing the Japanese internment, John Sanford writes, "It would not be long before the old ones sat gazing off into the distance as if there were nothing near they cared to see."

BACKGROUND

In *The Winters of That Country: Tales of the Man-Made Seasons,* John Sanford uses vignettes—short descriptive sketches—to portray important moments in United States history. Students often complain that they find their history textbooks dull and, as a result, difficult to read. After students have read this passage by Sanford, ask them to read the section in their American history textbook describing the Japanese internment camps and then compare this presentation of facts with John Sanford's vignette.

FOR DISCUSSION AND REFLECTION

➤ Why do you think John Sanford chooses to describe the interned Japanese Americans as "goods in motion"? (Students should consider how when people are dehumanized and considered merchandise, it makes it easier to treat them badly.)

➤ How does Sanford's description of infants that "wilt and die, blistered by blown sand" make you feel? (Many responses are possible, but Sanford is purposely appealing to our senses and our sense of outrage at this unnecessary suffering.)

➤ According to Sandford's account, what is happening to the old ones? (They have become disheartened by present circumstances and would travel in their minds: "somewhere in the far blue mountains: their past, the best of life, was there.")

➤ How is the children's response to internment different? (They continued to live in the present with its "sand-burs to burn, thistle, arrowgrass, and there'd be a need to learn and wait.")

➤ What does Sanford's vignette predict will happen to these innocent children who have been kept behind wire fences? (One day when they realize the injustice that had been done to them, "they'd begin to hate: what happened would happen to them.")

Writing

QUICK ASSESS

Do students' drawings:

✓ picture the scene which Sanford describes?

✓ convey their impressions of the piece?

Students are asked to sketch the picture that John Sanford's words have created in their minds. Remind students that the object is not to create a work of beauty here but rather to translate the words on the page into images.

READING AND WRITING EXTENSIONS

➤ Encourage students to read another vignette from John Sanford's collection, one about a moment in history with which they are familiar. Ask them to compare his portrayal with their own point of view regarding this event.

➤ Have students write a vignette describing a scene they know well: students waiting at a bus stop, football players in a huddle, teenagers at a dance.

Five Fictionalizing History

Critical Reading

FOCUS
Using omniscient narrators and stream of consciousness helps writers dramatize their stories.

BACKGROUND
An omniscient narrator gives readers access to the thoughts and feelings of all the characters. (*Omniscient* means "all-knowing.") It is through omniscience that the reader becomes aware of what any given character is like behind his or her outward mannerisms. This is the point of view David Guterson has used in *Snow Falling on Cedars*. He also employs stream of consciousness to take the reader inside the mind of Hatsue. This technique, made famous by James Joyce in his novel *Ulysses*, attempts to express the inner thought process directly, incorporating unedited the character's incidental thoughts and stray observations.

FOR DISCUSSION AND REFLECTION
➤ What inferences can you draw from the list of things that Hatsue says are "cluttering her heart"? (The story takes place just before Executive Order 9066 has been decreed. The boy she loves is about to be drafted in order to fight the Japanese. She herself is Japanese American.)

➤ In what ways is Hatsue like teenagers you know? (Answers may include her feelings about her mother, her boyfriend, and her feelings about who she is.)

➤ What does Guterson's use of stream of consciousness allow readers to know about Hatsue? (Readers have access to her uncensored thoughts.)

Writing

QUICK ASSESS
Do students' narratives:

✔ use an omniscient narrator?

✔ use stream of consciousness effectively?

Students are asked to use an omniscient narrator to dramatize the situation they wrote about in the first three lessons. Ask for a volunteer to allow you to use his or her first-person account as a model for demonstrating how to turn this into a third-person narrative.

READING AND WRITING EXTENSIONS
➤ Have students sit quietly for fifteen minutes and try to record their own stream of consciousness. Tell them to write without concern that anyone else will see what they have written.

➤ Ask students to research the history of the internment of Japanese Americans during World War II. Have them discuss how this additional information influences their interpretation of the texts they have read in Lessons One through Five.

STORY STRUCTURES

Unit Overview

In this unit, students focus on the choices writers make in structuring their stories. As they read and respond to fiction by Tennessee Williams, Ralph Ellison, and Thomas Wolfe, students explore the connections between beginnings and endings, the effects of foreshadowing, the use of flashbacks, and the methods by which the unity of a story is achieved.

Literature Focus

Lesson	Literature
1. As the Story Begins and Ends	**Tennessee Williams,** "A Lady's Beaded Bag" (Short Story)
2. Suspense Through Foreshadowing	
3. Flashbacks	**Ralph Ellison,** from "Flying Home" (Short Story)
4. The Fork in the Road	**Thomas Wolfe,** "The Far and the Near" (Short Story)
5. Unity in the Story	

Reading Focus

1. The beginning of a story prepares the reader for whatever experiences and actions follow. The ending shows the significance of even the smallest detail, image, or action.

2. Foreshadowing is a structural device used to create suspense and maintain the reader's involvement in the story.

3. Flashbacks break up the plot sequence of a story by moving into the past to provide relevant information or explanation.

4. Writers structure a story so that readers can understand what shapes a character. Most stories include a crucial point at which, or after which, a character's choices become significantly diminished.

5. As readers begin to sense the pattern or design of the story, they can begin to see the relationships between various elements of the plot and character.

Writing Focus

1. Examine a story's beginning and ending.
2. Identify and analyze examples of foreshadowing.
3. Explain a flashback and tell how it reveals character.
4. Write an interior dialogue for a character.
5. Sketch two scenes from a short story.

One As the Story Begins and Ends

Critical Reading

FOCUS

It is difficult to resist reading a short story with an intriguing opening sentence like, "Through the chill of a November evening a small man trudged down an alley, bearing upon his shoulders a huge, bulging sack."

BACKGROUND

Tennessee Williams is best known for his plays that reveal a world of human frustration where sex and violence are just under the surface of romantic gentility. The short story "A Lady's Beaded Bag" depicts a down-and-out scavenger who has finally found the treasure he has long hoped for, "something for which he might receive hundreds of dollars, bringing the fulfillment of his beggar-dreams." But when he mistakenly thinks that his treasure, a lady's beaded bag, has been missed and a chauffeur sent to find it, the trash-picker returns the purse to its rightful owner. The reader discovers that the owner never noticed or cared that it had been lost. When presented with the bill for a new dress, this frivolous woman tosses the several hundred dollars contained in the beaded bag—a fortune to the scavenger—to her maid to pay for the dress: "'Honestly, I must have been out of my mind when I bought this thing. Why I could never dream of wearing anything so perfectly ridiculous.'"

FOR DISCUSSION AND REFLECTION

➤ What clues to the trash-picker's character can you find in the opening paragraph? (His manner "seemed to indicate a sense of guilt and fear of detection." He is "oppressed with an almost maniacal sense of lowliness and shame.")

➤ How do these habits and traits make plausible his return of the beaded bag? (Answers are likely to include a discussion of the scavenger as a loser, someone who is so afraid of getting kicked by the world that he inevitably does: "He moved with that uneasy, half-unconscious stealth characteristic of an old and weary mongrel . . . .")

➤ Why does the owner of the beaded bag stand in such contrast to his character? (She is everything he is not— rich, carefree, careless with her possessions, cared for by others, utterly self-centered and self-satisfied.)

Writing

QUICK ASSESS

Do students' charts:

✓ list important details from the beginning?

✓ explain how details are reintroduced?

✓ connect the details to the story's meaning?

Students are asked to chart how the beginning and the end of the story work together. Before they begin, be sure that students understand the ironic nature of the ending wherein the honest weak man is discarded while the vain rich woman turns back to her mirror.

READING AND WRITING EXTENSIONS

➤ Have students write about a time when they were punished for doing the right thing.

➤ Encourage students to write a new ending for the story. Have them replace the last paragraph about the rich woman with one that turns again to the thoughts and actions of the trash-picker.

Two Suspense Through Foreshadowing

Critical Reading

FOCUS

Foreshadowing is the narrative device of planting hints and suggestions that anticipate significant upcoming events.

BACKGROUND

The short story tends to move toward what Edgar Allan Poe called "the single effect," a culmination that pulls together and resolves the tensions created by the characters and their circumstances. For all the diverse options open to writers, most stories still conform to a classic short story form with the beginning, middle, and end coming in natural sequence. There is exposition in which the characters and their situations are introduced, followed by rising action which poses and then intensifies the complications building toward a climax. The climax is the moment of greatest tension, a point after which the circumstances must change. After the climax comes the resolution or falling action that shows the consequences.

➤ Stories like Tennessee Williams's hold our attention by creating an atmosphere of suspense around the characters and events. We read on because we want to learn what happens next. Suspense creates expectation through the holding back of information. When the trash-picker reaches into the milliner's box, we wonder what he will find inside. When he returns the beaded bag to the owner, we wonder if he will be punished or rewarded.

FOR DISCUSSION AND REFLECTION

➤ Ask students to share the passages they have identified as foreshadowing and to explain the effect this hint had upon their reading of the story. (The first paragraph is full of descriptive details about the trash-picker that suggest he will never find the prize he seeks or that even should he find it, as he does with the lady's beaded bag, that he would be likely to lose it.)

➤ Why do you think the ending of this story does not come as a surprise? (Astute readers will have inferred from Williams's description of the trash-picker how this adventure was likely to turn out for him.)

➤ The story concludes with Mrs. Ferrabye smiling in self-satisfaction. What do you think the trash-picker's face looks like at this moment? (Answers will likely include a description of dismay and self-loathing.)

Writing

QUICK ASSESS

Do students' charts:

✓ identify foreshadowing in the story?

✓ recognize the effect foreshadowing has upon readers?

Students are asked to chart the techniques employed in this story to create foreshadowing. Complete one box together on the board for students to use as a model for their own.

READING AND WRITING EXTENSIONS

➤ Have students read the short story "Dr. Heidegger's Experiment" and discuss how Nathaniel Hawthorne has used foreshadowing to create suspense.

➤ Invite students to write about how Williams's foreshadowing would have to change if the story ended with the trash-picker being handsomely rewarded for returning the lady's beaded bag.

Three Flashbacks

Critical Reading

FOCUS

A flashback is a literary technique that involves interrupting the chronological sequence of events by interjecting events or scenes of earlier occurrence.

BACKGROUND

Ralph Ellison won the National Book Award in 1953 for his novel *Invisible Man*. As a child, Ellison was an avid reader. The books and magazines that his mother brought home from the white households where she worked as a domestic opened up new worlds for him: "You might say that my environment was extended by these slender threads into the worlds of white families. These magazines spoke to me of a life that was broader and more interesting and although it was not really a part of my own life, I never thought they were not for me because I happened to be a Negro. They were things which spoke of a world which I could some day make my own."

FOR DISCUSSION AND REFLECTION

➤ Why do you think that the narrator and pilot, Todd, flashes back to his childhood? (Many answers are possible, but students are likely to see a relationship between the crash of his airplane and his first sight of a plane as a small child. In pain, his mind turns away from the present to a happier past. Also, the narrator scans the sky for planes both in the past and in the present.)

➤ In the first paragraph, set in the story's present, the narrator refers to "the screen of pain." In the final paragraph of the flashback, Todd describes opening a screen and falling, expecting to be able to grasp the plane in the sky. Can you see a connection between these two "screens"? (Both act as dividing lines between two worlds: in the first, between consciousness and unconsciousness; in the second, between a child's fantasy and the actual physical world.)

➤ How would your parents have responded if you kept pestering them for something the way Todd badgered his mother? (Responses will vary.)

Writing

QUICK ASSESS

Do students' charts:

✓ identify passages about Todd's current situation?

✓ explain how they reveal character?

Students are asked to identify passages that inform readers about Todd's current situation and to explain how the passages help readers better understand his character. Before they begin, have students list character traits that they feel Todd possesses.

READING AND WRITING EXTENSIONS

➤ Have students describe an object that they remember wanting badly, perhaps even obsessively, as a child.

➤ Read students the prologue to *Invisible Man* and discuss what Ellison means when he calls himself an invisible man: "I am an invisible man. No, I am not a spook like those who haunted Edgar Allan Poe; nor am I one of your Hollywood-movie ectoplasms. I am a man of substance, of flesh and bone, fiber and liquids—and I might even be said to possess a mind. I am invisible, understand, simply because people refuse to see me."

Four The Fork in the Road

Critical Reading

FOCUS

Plot is what arises the moment the character, or characters, are set into motion.

BACKGROUND

E.M. Forster observed that if we write, "The king died, and the queen died," we have a narrative, but if we write instead, "The king died, and the queen died of grief," then we have a plot. The second statement establishes a link of causality between the two events. A narrative simply records events. For a narrative to become a plot, it must reveal its meaning in human terms. Events only become interesting when we see their effect upon people. In "The Far and the Near," Thomas Wolfe leaves the task of interpreting events to the reader. We are told that the engineer passed by the house of a woman who, though unknown to him, waved to him each day "a few minutes after two o'clock in the afternoon." When he retires, the man decides to pay a visit to the woman. The meeting is not a success. The plot of "The Far and the Near" depends upon the reader making the necessary inferences and the connections.

FOR DISCUSSION AND REFLECTION

➤ What did the woman who waved represent to the engineer through all those twenty years? (Responses are likely to include reference to a sense of an ordered, wholesome life, cheerful and dependable: "The vision of the little house and the women waving to him with a brave free motion of the arm had become fixed in the mind of the engineer as something beautiful and enduring, something beyond all change and ruin . . . .")

➤ Why does the engineer have misgivings on the way to visit the woman? (Up close, everything about the town was shabbier than he had imagined from a distance: "It was all as unfamiliar, as disquieting as a city in a dream . . . .")

➤ Why could the magic never return? (Once the engineer had seen the "ugly little parlor" and the sullen woman, he could never recapture the vision of what he had imagined, what she had represented for him all those years.)

Writing

QUICK ASSESS

Do students' dialogues:

✓ imagine what the engineer might be thinking and feeling?

✓ explain his reasons for visiting the women?

Students are asked to write an interior monologue for the engineer. Help them establish a point in time when the engineer would be having these thoughts, possibly on his way home from his visit to the little house.

READING AND WRITING EXTENSIONS

➤ Have students write about a time when something they had imagined from a distance as wonderful turned out to be quite the opposite up close.

➤ Have students describe the visit from the woman's point of view. Have her explain why she waved all those times and how the engineer's visit affected her.

Five Unity in the Story

Critical Reading

FOCUS

Aristotle's prescription for Greek tragedy held that there were certain "unities"—of time, of place, and of action.

BACKGROUND

In *The Art of Fiction*, John Gardner wrote, "In great fiction we are moved by what happens, not by the whimpering or bawling of the writer's presentation of what happens. That is, in great fiction, we are moved by characters and events, not by the emotion of the person who happens to be telling the story. When ideas, characters, and actions are firmly grounded, Thomas Wolfe's or William Faulkner's style can give fitting expression to a story's emotional content."

➤ "The Far and the Near" is given a sense of unity by the story's emotional content. The engineer knows that now that he has seen the little house and the woman who was an icon for him up close, he will never be able to recover the vision of how he imagined them to be from a distance. Explain to students Aristotle's unities and discuss how Wolfe has conformed to them in this story. Unity of time means that the action should not take place over more than a twenty-four-hour time period. Unity of place means that the locale is usually confined to a single city. Unity of action means that the plot focuses upon the central conflict and avoid confusing subplots.

FOR DISCUSSION AND REFLECTION

➤ How does the point of view from which this story is told influence your reading of it? (Answers are likely to include a discussion of how the third-person narrator keeps the reader at a distance from the emotions that the engineer is feeling and allows the reader to be objective about what occurs.)

➤ How would you characterize Thomas Wolfe's style? (Have students support their varying answers with examples of specific phrases and sentences from the story.)

➤ What insight into the human condition do you take away from the story? (There is no one correct answer, but students should focus on the way the engineer's vision of the world has shifted as a result of seeing the little house and the woman up close.)

Writing

QUICK ASSESS

Do students' sketches:

✔ reflect understanding of how Wolfe's title emphasizes his theme?

✔ depict scenes from the beginning and the end?

Students are asked to write about how Wolfe's title emphasizes the way he structured continuity into the story and then to sketch two important scenes.

READING AND WRITING EXTENSIONS

➤ Have students describe the experience of seeing someone or something on television or in a movie and then seeing the person, place, or thing again themselves, up close.

➤ Read to students Amy Clampitt's poem "Fog," which moves from blurriness to precision and back to blurriness. Have them discuss whether or not her description of the world as seen through a fog is similar to the engineer's experience of the little house and woman as seen from a moving train.

Unit Overview

In "Talking Back in Poetry," students will learn to appreciate how knowledge about a poem's time and culture can deepen their understanding and increase their enjoyment as they read. Students consider the ways in which a poet refers to other poems through focusing on allusion and parodies as they read works by poets such as Langston Hughes, Walt Whitman, and William Carlos Williams.

Literature Focus

	Lesson	Literature
1.	Historical and Cultural Perspectives	**Langston Hughes,** "I, Too, Sing America" (Poetry)
2.	Understanding Allusions	**Walt Whitman,** "I Hear America Singing" (Poetry)
3.	Analyzing Allusions	**Sara Henderson Hay,** "One of the Seven Has Somewhat to Say" (Poetry)
4.	Talking Back with Parody	**William Carlos Williams,** "This Is Just to Say" (Poetry) **Kenneth Koch,** "Variations on a Theme by William Carlos Williams" (Poetry)
5.	Analyzing a Parody	

Reading Focus

1. Knowing the era and culture of a poem provides an additional perspective for understanding the meaning.
2. Knowing that a poet is alluding to a previous work provides an additional perspective for understanding both poems.
3. A poet can use an allusion to make a statement about contemporary attitudes.
4. A good writer of parodies must understand and appreciate the original. An active reader needs to understand how the two works compare and contrast to understand the parody.
5. Writing a parody is another way that poets talk back to each other. Parodies follow the style of the original but also comment on it.

Writing Focus

1. Explain a line of a poem.
2. Write about how a poem uses an allusion to another poem.
3. Argue a point about a poem, drawing on specific text evidence as support.
4. Use a Venn diagram to compare two poems, one a parody of the other.
5. Analyze a poem's structure.

One Historical and Cultural Perspectives

Critical Reading

FOCUS

Active readers make an effort to understand how a writer's culture influences his or her work.

BACKGROUND

Langston Hughes was the acknowledged leader of the Harlem Renaissance, beginning in 1917 and running through 1935. It was a new African-American movement in the arts and letters, and Hughes was in the middle of it. He began writing poetry in grammar school when he was elected class poet by his fellow students. By age nineteen, he had already begun publishing in magazines, but was still not nationally known. The story is told that Hughes first won national recognition while working as a busboy in a restaurant where the poet Vachel Lindsay ate. One day Hughes slipped three poems beside Lindsay's plate, and the next morning the papers reported that Lindsay had found a great talent. Langston Hughes then became known as the Poet Laureate of Harlem. His work has influenced generations of writers. According to Hughes, "The rhythms of poetry give continuity and pattern to words, to thoughts, strengthening them, adding the qualities of permanence, and relating the written words to the vast rhythms of life."

FOR DISCUSSION AND REFLECTION

➤ What do you feel this poem is saying about America? (Answers should include discussion of how African Americans were for many years excluded from "the table" in America.)

➤ How would you describe the narrator's attitude towards this state of affairs? (He seems confident that America will come to its senses and, realizing his strength and beauty, invite him to the table. The poem celebrates an America that is inclusive rather than exclusive.)

➤ What is the narrator's strategy for moving from the kitchen to the table when "company comes"? (He says he will "laugh, / And eat well, / And grow strong." The lines suggest that the narrator is aware of his own accruing power and certain of his right to be there.)

Writing

QUICK ASSESS

Do students' responses:

✔ reflect a thoughtful understanding of the poem?

✔ explain the meaning of Hughes's statement?

Students are asked to explain what they think Hughes meant by "They'll see how beautiful I am / And be ashamed—" Before they write, discuss the possible things that America has to be ashamed of in the history of African Americans.

READING AND WRITING EXTENSIONS

➤ Read students Zora Neale Hurston's essay "How It Feels To Be Colored Me." Ask them to compare this Harlem Renaissance writer's image of herself with that portrayed in "I, Too, Sing America."

➤ Teenagers often feel like outsiders. Ask students to write a poem about themselves and their own experiences of feeling left out using Hughes's first line, "I, Too, Sing America," as their own.

Two Understanding Allusions

C r i t i c a l   R e a d i n g

FOCUS

Through the use of allusion a poet can respond to what others have written.

BACKGROUND

Walt Whitman revolutionized American literature. Whitman held a great variety of jobs, from printer to teacher to nurse in the Civil War. He spent much of his time when not at work walking and observing in New York City. The poems in *Leaves of Grass* address the citizens of the United States, urging them to be large and generous in spirit, a new race nurtured in political liberty. His lines are long and rambling, like the expanding country. His language reflects the vigor and energy of American speech, resounding with new, distinctively American rhythms. Walt Whitman's poetry is full of optimism, vitality, and a love of nature, free expression, and democracy—values often associated with the America of his day.

FOR DISCUSSION AND REFLECTION

➤ What do you think "singing" represents in this poem? (Possible responses include the simple pleasure a worker can take from a job well done, as well as an expression of the importance of manual labor to America's growth and success.)

➤ How would you describe Walt Whitman's view of America? (Whitman sees America as peopled by hard-working, happy people. He recognizes that these workers are the lifeblood of this country. He paints a joyous, egalitarian picture of America.)

➤ Is Hughes's or Whitman's picture of America closer to your own? (Ask students to explain their answers with examples from their experience and from the poems.)

W r i t i n g

QUICK ASSESS

Do students' responses:

✓ analyze the two poems?

✓ explore Hughes's use of the allusion to the Whitman poem?

Students are asked to explain what they perceive Langston Hughes to be saying to Walt Whitman and the world of readers by his allusion. Discuss how Langston Hughes's experience of America was likely to have been quite different from Walt Whitman's experience.

READING AND WRITING EXTENSIONS

➤ Lorraine Hansberry's play *A Raisin in the Sun* takes its title from a line in the Langston Hughes poem "Harlem": "What happens to a dream deferred? / Does it dry up / like a raisin in the sun? / or fester like a sore— / And then run? / Does it stink like rotten meat? / Or crust and sugar over — / like a syrupy sweet? / Maybe it just sags / like a heavy load. / Or does it explode?" Have students choose a line from either the Walt Whitman poem or the Langston Hughes poem and use it as the title of their own poems about America.

➤ Read students Carl Sandburg's poem "Chicago" and have them compare his portrait of the city with Whitman's view of America as expressed in "I Hear America Singing."

Three Analyzing Allusions

Critical Reading

FOCUS

An allusion is a writer's indirect reference to another work with which he or she hopes the reader will be acquainted.

BACKGROUND

After they read and discuss the poem, students may need to be reminded of the story of Snow White and the Seven Dwarfs in order to understand the allusions that Sara Henderson Hay is making. Most likely many of them will have been exposed only to the Walt Disney version of this story. If possible, read them "Little Snow-White" from *Grimm's Fairy Tales*. After Snow White had told the seven little men about her wicked stepmother, "The Dwarfs said, 'Will you see after our household; be our cook, make the beds, wash, sew, and knit for us, and keep everything in neat order? If so, we will keep you here, and you shall want for nothing.' And Snow-White answered, 'Yes, with all my heart and will.' And so she remained with them, and kept their house in order." Sara Henderson Hay has used one of the seven dwarfs to comment on the ways many men view women's domestic habits.

FOR DISCUSSION AND REFLECTION

➤ When did you first begin to recognize that the poem was making an allusion to Snow White and the Seven Dwarfs? (Have students identify the specific places in the poem that offer clues.)

➤ How does the speaker of this poem feel about the presence of Snow White in his life? (Answers should include a discussion of his resentment of the order that she has brought to their lives and a longing for the good old days. Make sure students recognize the author's viewpoint as separate from that of the speaker.)

➤ What do you think will happen in this household when Snow White departs? (Encourage students to think about how their different answers reflect assumptions that they have about how men and women differ in their domestic habits.)

Writing

QUICK ASSESS

Do students' paragraphs:

✓ support one of the two sentences?

✓ cite specific text evidence?

Students are asked to choose one of two statements about the poem and to write in support of its premise. Remind students to offer specific supporting evidence in the form of quotes from the text.

READING AND WRITING EXTENSIONS

➤ Have students choose a minor character from a fairy tale that they know well and write an interior monologue expressing how this person feels about the hero or heroine.

➤ Read students Anne Sexton's poem "Self in 1958" and have them compare the speaker's portrayal of herself as a plaster doll with the dwarf's portrayal of Snow White in "One of the Seven Has Somewhat to Say."

Four Talking Back with Parody

Critical Reading

FOCUS

A parody is a literary work in which the style of an author is closely imitated either for the purpose of comic effect or for ridicule.

BACKGROUND

William Carlos Williams succeeded in making the ordinary appear extraordinary through the clarity of his imagery. Williams was a practicing physician and often wrote poems on the back of a prescription pad or on odd pieces of paper he found in his pocket. This particular poem was, in fact, an actual note left on a refrigerator door that he wrote to a friend he was staying with after having returned late and consumed his plums. Critics lambasted the poem when it first appeared, accusing it of being no more than a casual throw-away piece of writing. Over time, readers have come to value it as an almost perfect piece, the kind of thing that only someone who had spent practically his whole life as a poet could write so naturally.

FOR DISCUSSION AND REFLECTION

➤ Do you believe the narrator of "This Is Just to Say" is sorry for having eaten the plums? (Though the narrator formally apologizes for the deed, he describes the pleasure he took in eating them so enthusiastically that the reader begins to doubt the authenticity of his regret.)

➤ What has Kenneth Koch preserved from the original in his "Variations on a Theme by William Carlos Williams"? (In each stanza he apologizes for an act that he is not much sorry for having committed, making flimsy excuses that demonstrate his lack of remorse.)

➤ How has Kenneth Koch diverged from Williams's model? (Instead of one almost crystalline moment, Koch offers readers a series of increasingly wacky deeds committed by an unrepentant narrator.)

Writing

QUICK ASSESS

Do students' diagrams:

✓ identify several specific similarities between the poems?

✓ identify several specific differences?

Before students work on their Venn diagrams comparing the two poems, read the Koch poem aloud, paying special attention to possible tones of voice one could use.

READING AND WRITING EXTENSIONS

➤ Have students write a letter to a friend unfamiliar with William Carlos Williams's work explaining what they find unique in his poetry. They may choose to recommend further reading of Williams's poetry or discourage it, but in either case should explain why.

➤ Read students Williams's poem "So Much Depends" and ask them to talk about what this "it" is that depends so much upon the red wheelbarrow.

Five Analyzing a Parody

Critical Reading

FOCUS

A parody may or may not follow the style and the structure of the original.

BACKGROUND

Kenneth Koch is noted for his witty, often surreal, poetry. His work is often whimsical. In the first stanza of "Variations on a Theme by William Carlos Williams," the narrator pretends to apologize for chopping down someone's house simply because he was bored. In the second, he demolishes the hollyhocks with lye and then excuses himself by saying that he doesn't know what he is doing. In the third, he gives away someone's life savings when a beggar asks for it, blaming his action upon the "juicy and cold" March wind. In the final stanza, he breaks his lover's leg in order to keep her in the hospital where he is a doctor. However dastardly the deeds being described, the tone of the narration remains light-hearted.

FOR DISCUSSION AND REFLECTION

➤ How does a careful reading of "Variations on a Theme by William Carlos Williams" cause you to see the Williams poem differently? (Answers may include a discussion of how Koch points out the self-satisfied nature of the narrator's apology in "This Is Just to Say.")

➤ Why do you think Koch calls the March wind "so juicy and cold"? (He purposely borrows this phrase from Williams's poem to point out that eating the plums just because they were juicy and cold is no more justification than his own distribution of money that was not his own and then blaming his action on the wind.)

➤ What do you think Kenneth Koch wants you to think or feel when you read his poem? (Responses will vary. Koch is clearly having fun with the poem.)

Writing

QUICK ASSESS

Do students' charts:

✓ select relevant details from Koch's parody?

✓ explain Koch's use of exaggeration in his variations?

Students are asked to chart the details used by Koch in his parody of "This Is Just to Say" and then to explain how he has made use of exaggeration for comic effect. To check that students understand exaggeration, have them discuss comic movies where exaggeration made them laugh.

READING AND WRITING EXTENSIONS

➤ Have students write a parody of "This Is Just to Say" in which they apologize for something that they are not really sorry for having done—for example, for having borrowed the calculator of their rival in math class or for having "liberated" a neighbor's squawking pet bird.

➤ William Carlos Williams often wrote poems that were directly related to personal experience. Read students "Danse Russe" and ask them to discuss how the speaker's solitary dance seems to be inspired by the famous Russian ballet company.

Unit Overview

"Modern Interpretations of Myth" provides students with an opportunity to explore how poets have used familiar myths. As they read and analyze works by Dorothy Parker, Edna St. Vincent Millay, Margaret Atwood, Rita Dove, and Muriel Rukeyser, students will learn how writers reinterpret older stories, place them in contemporary settings, and shift their point of view.

Literature Focus

	Lesson	Literature
1.	Paying Attention to the Title	**Dorothy Parker,** "Penelope" (Poetry)
2.	Making Connections	**Edna St. Vincent Millay,** "An Ancient Gesture" (Poetry)
3.	Ancient Myths in Modern Dress	**Margaret Atwood,** "Siren Song" (Poetry)
4.	Changing the Tone of a Myth	**Rita Dove,** "Demeter's Prayer to Hades" (Poetry)
5.	Changing Perspective	**Muriel Rukeyser,** "Myth" (Poetry)

Reading Focus

1. The title of a poem is essential for placing the reader in the world of the poem. It is often the reader's best clue to what the poet is commenting on.

2. It is important to recognize when a writer is employing an older story or a myth in a poem. Knowing the original allows you to see how the writer is reinterpreting and commenting on older stories.

3. Contemporary language makes it easy for us to see the meaning of a myth in our own times.

4. Do not be misled by the apparent subject of a poem. Look for the tone of the poem to give you insight into the possibilities of meaning in poetry.

5. Changing point of view or perspective can give you new insights into well-known stories.

Writing Focus

1. Answer questions about a poem's title and meaning.
2. Compare two poems about Penelope, the wife of Odysseus.
3. Analyze a poem's language and meaning.
4. Rewrite a poem line by line.
5. Compose a poetic monologue.

One Paying Attention to the Title

Critical Reading

FOCUS

Titles often provide significant clues to a poem's meaning.

BACKGROUND

Unlike Penelope, who was famous for her patience and faithfulness, Dorothy Parker was famous for saying what was on her mind. Her biting, clever jibes are literary legend. In a letter to a friend she once wrote, "Dear God, please make me stop writing like a woman." For Parker, "writing like a woman" meant thinking like one who is bound to the ideals of home and romantic love. In "Penelope," Parker uses characters from *The Odyssey* to critique the traditional roles played by men and women. Men like Odysseus get to "ride the silver seas" and "cut the glittering wave," while women like Penelope must "sit at home, and rock."

➤ The final line suggests that bravery should not be measured only by glamorous deeds but also by steadfast service. According to Parker, "In all history, which has held billions and billions of human beings, not a single one ever had a happy ending."

FOR DISCUSSION AND REFLECTION

➤ If you judge by the tone of this poem, how do you think the speaker feels about sitting at home and rocking? (Penelope seems to be saying that Odysseus's life of adventure has all the glamour while hers is full of toil.)

➤ What does the speaker imply by saying that, "They will call him brave"? (Read this line aloud with an almost sarcastic emphasis on the word *him*. Penelope is saying that Odysseus's bold deeds earn him fame while her labors receive little recognition.)

➤ How is Parker's poem a commentary on contemporary roles in marriage? (Many responses are possible and will be influenced by students' experiences of working mothers, stay-at-home-dads, celebrity parents, and so forth.)

➤ Why do you think Dorothy Parker chose a couple from mythology to critique contemporary relationships? (Penelope is a symbol of faithful devotion and long-suffering patience. Odysseus is the ultimate adventurer, always on the lookout for the next horizon. References to well-known stories from mythology allow a poet to speak to readers without much explanation.)

Writing

QUICK ASSESS

Do students' answers:

✓ reflect a thoughtful reading of the poem?

✓ explain the title's significance?

✓ explain the poem's message?

Students are asked to answer questions about the poem, including one about the poem's meaning. Remind students that there is no one right answer, that they are reaching for a thoughtful explanation that can be supported with evidence from the text.

READING AND WRITING EXTENSIONS

➤ Have students research other poems by Dorothy Parker and share with the class those that have messages similar to that of "Penelope."

➤ Have students try to think of other titles for Parker's poem that would hint at the meaning they think the author is trying to get across.

Two Making Connections

Critical Reading

FOCUS
Penelope represents the faithful wife, prudent and resourceful in the difficult position in which she has been placed by her husband's long absence.

BACKGROUND
In "An Ancient Gesture," the speaker uses the classical story of Penelope and her nineteen-year wait for Odysseus to make sense of her own waiting and particularly of her own weeping. In the first stanza, the speaker compares herself with Penelope, recalling this peerless wife's cunning ploy to put off the suitors. The narrator imagines how tired Penelope's arms and neck must have grown weaving and unraveling, waiting without knowing where Odysseus was or when he might return: "Suddenly you burst into tears; / There is simply nothing else to do." In the second stanza, the speaker reflects upon how this weeping—both her own and Penelope's—is an ancient gesture, "authentic, antique, / In the very best tradition, classic, Greek . . . ." Of course, Odysseus was known for his weeping, too, but the narrator discounts this as a feeble gesture, one he knew how to use to effect and had learned from his wife. The poem concludes with the assumption that, despite all Odysseus's travel and trouble, it is Penelope who has done the real suffering.

FOR DISCUSSION AND REFLECTION
➤ Why do you think Millay chose to have the speaker in the poem address Penelope directly? (Addressing Penelope as "you" makes the poem a conversation with a mythological figure. The narrator is looking to Penelope for assurance that her tears are not a sign of weakness. The poem also assumes that she, Penelope, and the reader are contemporaries.)

➤ What effect does the repetition of the first line of the poem in the second stanza have upon you? (Answers will likely include a discussion of how the speaker is reminding the reader that she is crying, wiping "my eyes on the corner of my apron . . . ." Tears are a central motif in the poem representing the suffering of one who waits.)

➤ How are Penelope's tears different from those of Odysseus? (Hers are genuine; his are for effect.)

Writing

QUICK ASSESS
Do students' comparisons:

✓ identify similarities between the two poems?

✓ identify differences between the two poems?

✓ explain which they find more effective?

Students are asked to compare Millay's poem with Dorothy Parker's and to write about their similarities and differences. It may help students to make a list on the board of the ways in which the two poems are alike and different.

READING AND WRITING EXTENSIONS
➤ Bring in reproductions of paintings from Pablo Picasso's "Weeping Women" series and have students write about how they, too, portray weeping as an ancient gesture.

➤ Read to students from Book IV of The Odyssey where Athena reassures Penelope: "So she spoke, and lulled Penelope's laments, and made her eyes to cease from weeping."

Three Ancient Myths in Modern Dress

Critical Reading

FOCUS

The song the Sirens tailored for Odysseus appealed to his unquenchable thirst for knowledge and still has meaning for contemporary readers:

"Come hither, as you farest, renowned Odysseus; stay thy ship that thou mayest listen. We know all the things that come to pass upon the fruitful earth."

BACKGROUND

The Sirens were fabulous creatures who had the power of drawing men to destruction with their song. To escape their lure and yet hear their song, Odysseus, when his ship was about to pass their island, filled the ears of his men with wax and had himself lashed to the mast. According to legend, the Sirens tailored their songs for the listener. In "Siren Song," the speaker is a Siren who addresses her listener in the second person. In her song she pretends to portray herself as someone in desperate need of help from her victim. She says she is tired of her "bird suit" and no longer enjoys "squatting on this island / looking picturesque and mythical . . . ." She calls her companions "feathery maniacs." The siren explains to her female audience the secret of her song—that the most seductive call of all is the one that manipulates a man by playing to his ego, his sense of being superior to women. Ironically, it is still valid today.

FOR DISCUSSION AND REFLECTION

➤ How does Atwood's use of "you" to represent the Siren's prey affect your reading of the poem? (The second-person reference puts readers in a vulnerable position. Like the "you" in the poem, readers are taken in by the Siren's song.)

➤ What is seductive about this particular Siren song? (She appeals to her listener's vanity and self-importance. If only he can set her free, then he must be quite a man.)

➤ Do you agree with the Siren's assumption that everyone wants to learn this song? (Answers will vary. Discuss the pros and cons of having this kind of power.)

Writing

QUICK ASSESS

Do students' responses:

✓ recognize the mythological elements in Atwood's poem?

✓ explain the issue of manipulation?

✓ comment on the poem's language?

Students are asked to write about what they think Atwood is saying about men and women in our society. Before they begin, ask students to think of other examples in literature or film in which women have lured men to their destruction.

READING AND WRITING EXTENSIONS

➤ Have students describe the kind of song they think the Sirens might sing to them in order to lure the class to the perilous shore. Have them consider areas where they think teens may be vulnerable to manipulation.

➤ Circe is another classical temptress from *The Odyssey*. Read and discuss together Margaret Atwood's *Circe/Mud Poems*: "Is this what you would like me to be this mud woman? / Is this what I would like to be? It would be so simple. / It's the story that counts. No use telling me this isn't a story / or not the same story."

Four Changing the Tone of a Myth

Critical Reading

FOCUS

Rita Dove on the Demeter/Persephone cycle:

Its betrayal and regeneration "is ideally suited for the sonnet form since all three—mother-goddess, daughter-consort, and poet—are struggling to sing in their chains."

BACKGROUND

"Demeter's Prayer to Hades" is taken from Rita Dove's collection *Mother Love*. In it, the poet recalls the ancient Greek myth of Demeter and Persephone to examine the tenacity of love between mother and daughter. In an introduction, Dove writes, "The ancient story of Demeter and Persephone is a tale of a violated world. It is a modern dilemma as well—there comes a point when a mother can no longer protect her child, when the daughter must go her own way into womanhood." The poems in this collection are sonnets, partly in homage and counterpoint to Rainer Marie Rilke's *Sonnets to Orpheus*.

FOR DISCUSSION AND REFLECTION

➤ What do you think Demeter means when she says to Hades that she wishes for him to be "responsible for the lives we change"? (Hades has significantly changed Persephone's life, and while Demeter no longer wishes to return to the time before this change, she is urging Hades to recognize what he has done.)

➤ What contemporary applications do you see for this wish of Demeter? (Answers will likely include a discussion of how whenever we meddle in human life—for good or for evil—we bear responsibility for those we have influenced.)

➤ How do you interpret the phrase "There are no curses, only mirrors"? (Many responses are possible. Students should discuss the nature of curses and the nature of mirrors. If mirrors reflect what is before them, Hades's kidnapping of Demeter's daughter reflects what is inside him—as well as what is inside Persephone and Demeter.)

Writing

QUICK ASSESS

Do students' revisions:

✔ reflect a good understanding of Dove's poem?

✔ paraphrase each line of the poem?

Students are asked to rewrite Demeter's prayer to Hades line by line, putting what they read into their own words. Explain to students that paraphrasing a poem should be a free rendering. Encourage them to take liberties with Dove's lines.

READING AND WRITING EXTENSIONS

➤ Have students read other poems from *Mother Love*, including "Demeter, Waiting": "She is gone again and I will not bear / it, I will drag my grief through a winter / of my own making and refuse / any meadow that recycles itself into / hope."

➤ Ask students to use the story of Demeter and Persephone to write a poem about their own mothers or mother-figures. The poem could be about a time they were lost as a child or about how they feel now about the prospect of leaving home in the next few years.

Five Changing Perspective

Critical Reading

FOCUS

Looking at a text from several angles can change your perceptions of it.

BACKGROUND

Muriel Rukeyser found an audience for her poetry late in life through her teaching and in the younger generation of emerging women writers. The poet Anne Sexton wrote "Muriel, mother of everyone, flowing out like an infusion of blood into the body" in a note thanking Rukeyser for *The Speed of Darkness*. In "Myth," Rukeyser uses the myth of Oedipus and the Sphinx to comment on modern society's assumption that the generic term *man* of course includes *women*. She does not agree. Rukeyser disputes that what "Everyone knows" is true.

FOR DISCUSSION AND REFLECTION

➤ Why do you think Muriel Rukeyser chose a character that was a blind man? (Answers are likely to include reference to the fact that Oedipus is literally blind and that his blindness has been self-inflicted. Rukeyser posits that many modern men simply don't "see" how their assumptions about women's inclusion in any reference to "mankind" is unfounded, an example of how they do not see the world as it is.)

➤ A traditional interpretation of the Oedipus story is that no man may deny his fate. How does Rukeyser reinterpret the myth? (Her Sphinx suggests to Oedipus that he could have altered his fate had he paid more attention to the women in his life.)

➤ Oedipus asks the Sphinx why he didn't recognize his mother. Her answer may at first seem to make no sense, but how do you interpret her reply? (The Sphinx tells Oedipus that even when he could see, he was blind to the women in his life. Given his assumptions about how the world worked, his wife could not possibly be his mother, and so he would never recognize her.)

Writing

QUICK ASSESS

Do students' monologues:

✓ use the point of view of Hades?

✓ address an angry Demeter?

Students are asked to explain the abduction of Persephone from the point of view of Hades. Before they begin, discuss how mothers may be reluctant to give up their daughters and how they may suffer when separated from a child.

READING AND WRITING EXTENSIONS

➤ Have students read May Sarton's poem "The Muse as Medusa" and discuss how the poet has used myth to reflect upon her own character: "I turn your face around! It is my face. / That frozen rage is what I must explore— / Oh secret, self-enclosed, a ravaged place! / This is the gift I thank Medusa for."

➤ Have students write a poem that uses a well-known myth to depict a contemporary situation.

Unit Overview

In this unit, students will have the opportunity to practice modeling the idea and form of a poem. As they read poems by Edwin Arlington Robinson, Robert Frost, William Stafford, and Wallace Stevens and song lyrics by Paul Simon, they learn about ballads, sonnets, and blank verse and write poems based on the selections they have studied.

Literature Focus

Lesson	Literature
1. Modeling an Idea	**Edwin Arlington Robinson,** "Richard Cory" (Poetry)
2. From Poem to Song	**Paul Simon,** "Richard Cory" (Song)
3. Writing a Sonnet	**Robert Frost,** "Design" (Poetry)
4. Writing a Parallel Poem	**William Stafford,** "Traveling Through the Dark" (Poetry)
5. Modeling and Drawing	**Wallace Stevens,** "Thirteen Ways of Looking at a Blackbird" (Poetry)

Reading Focus

1. Modeling the idea and form of a poem requires paying close attention to the original poem.
2. A ballad has a musical rhythm and a refrain that repeats a central idea.
3. Word-for-word modeling is an exercise that helps a reader understand the skill of a poet.
4. Unrhymed iambic pentameter sounds like everyday speech. It is a meter commonly used in poetry because it is graceful but still simple.
5. Drawing can enhance the power of concrete images and details in both reading and writing.

Writing Focus

1. Write a poem based on a model.
2. Recast a poem into a song.
3. Write an emulation of a Robert Frost poem.
4. Use a model to write a poem in blank verse.
5. Write a poem about an object, drawing pictures to illustrate different ways it can be viewed.

One Modeling an Idea

Critical Reading

FOCUS

Writing from models requires careful reading and a willingness to play with language.

BACKGROUND

Edwin Arlington Robinson's "Richard Cory" is from a series of poems depicting the inner lives of people in Tilbury Town, a fictional community modeled on Robinson's hometown of Gardiner, Maine. Robinson said about "Richard Cory" that "There isn't any idealism in it, but there's lots of something else—humanity, maybe." The poem depicts a wealthy gentleman, "admirably schooled in every grace," who inspires envy in all the poorer townsfolk: "In fine, we thought that he was everything / To make us wish that we were in his place." The poem demonstrates no idealism because it offers no possible bridge between Cory and the townspeople. Its humanity lies in its acknowledgment of the difficulty that people who live in isolation feel, whatever their economic status.

➤ "Richard Cory" is written in iambic pentameter, which causes the poem to sound natural, almost conversational. A variation of the meter in the next to last line creates a pause and a tension that is released by the final line, which completes the rhyme scheme and gives shocking emphasis to the speaker's words.

FOR DISCUSSION AND REFLECTION

➤ How do the townspeople regard Richard Cory? (They admire, respect, and envy him. They do not understand him. Encourage students to find evidence in the poem for their answers.)

➤ Why do you think Richard Cory kills himself? (Answers should include discussion of how his demeanor suggests a person isolated by his own seemingly perfect life. The speaker repeatedly uses "we" to speak of the townspeople. However poor they may be, they have one another.)

➤ What do you think Robinson intended as the message of this poem? (Many responses are possible: One should not judge happiness by appearances, money does not buy personal satisfaction.)

Writing

QUICK ASSESS

Do students' poems:

✓ use "Richard Cory" as a model?

✓ include a final, surprising twist?

Students are asked to write a poem modeled on "Richard Cory" about a person who seems to have everything a teenager would want. As a class, make a list on the board of what these things might be. Help students to move from generalizations such as "beauty" or "money" to specifics such as "a BMW," "a Mastercard of her own," "the perfect nose."

READING AND WRITING EXTENSIONS

➤ Read to students Paul Laurence Dunbar's poem "We Wear the Mask" and have students compare the mask Richard Cory wore with the mask that Dunbar describes.

➤ Bring to class reproductions of Romare Beardon's collage portraits and invite students to create a portrait of themselves, with magazine clippings representing the various masks that they wear in the world.

Two From Poem to Song

Critical Reading

FOCUS

Paul Simon's song, based on Edwin Arlington Robinson's poem, offers the reader additional insight into the life of one of the poor townsfolk who work in Richard Cory's factory.

BACKGROUND

Songwriter Paul Simon took the Edwin Arlington Robinson poem "Richard Cory" and reshaped it as a song. In doing so he made several changes, some of them at the service of translating a poem to song, some of them at the service of his own point regarding the lives of poor working folks. The first obvious difference in the two poems is the presence of a refrain in the Paul Simon version. What is particularly effective about this refrain is how the same words take on a different meaning in the final stanza. Not only does the speaker wish he could be Richard Cory in life but also in death, suggesting that anything is preferable to the miserable life he is leading. "I curse the life I'm living / And I curse my poverty / And I wish that I could be / Richard Cory."

FOR DISCUSSION AND REFLECTION

➤ How has changing the narrator from plural to singular, "we" to "I," affected this version of "Richard Cory"? (Many responses are possible but should include discussion of how this narrator does not represent a collective poor folk, but instead one bitter and discouraged man's point of view.)

➤ How does the refrain take on new meaning in the final stanza after readers learn that Richard Cory has committed suicide? (The speaker in this poem so despises his own life that he continues to envy Richard Cory even in his death.)

➤ If Richard Cory had left a note behind, what do you think it might have said? (Answers should include reference to his own dissatisfaction with life, affluent and pleasurable as it seemed to be to others.)

Writing

QUICK ASSESS

Do students' songs:

✓ express understanding of Cory's life?

✓ include a refrain after each stanza?

Students are asked to adapt their poem from Lesson One into a song. Use one student's poem and have the class work together to write a refrain for it. This will give them a second model to use along with that of Paul Simon.

READING AND WRITING EXTENSIONS

➤ Bring in a recording of Paul Simon's "Richard Cory" and have students listen to how the music enhances his words. Then invite those who are so inclined to put their song to music and to perform it for the class.

➤ Have students write a dramatic scene from the life of Richard Cory, possibly using a narrator like the one employed by Edwin Arlington Robinson (a kind of Greek chorus) or the one used by Paul Simon.

Three Writing a Sonnet

Critical Reading

FOCUS
Emulating helps you understand an author's style as you create your own.

BACKGROUND

In many ways, Robert Frost is a transitional figure between the poets of the nineteenth and twentieth centuries. Like the transcendentalists before him, Frost loved nature and wrote about the lone individual deliberately making choices about how to live. Like the modernists who were his contemporaries, Frost wrote about the forces in modern society that isolate people. Many of his poems portray the tensions in relationships and the advantages and disadvantages of being alone. He uses the regional diction of New England, plain spoken, yet reserved, with a solidity like the land itself. His word choice is usually concrete and informal.

➤ In "Design," Frost uses the form of a sonnet in order to reflect upon meaning in nature. In the octave, he describes what he saw one morning: a spider atop a flower holding a dead moth: "Assorted characters of death and blight / Mixed ready to begin the morning right . . . ." In the sestet, Frost ponders why the natural world works in these particular ways. In the final couplet, he reflects on his own question, "What but design of darkness to appall?— / If design govern in a thing so small."

FOR DISCUSSION AND REFLECTION

➤ What do you think Frost intended by his juxtaposition of "characters of death and blight" with "begin the morning right"? (Answers should include discussion of the idea that though the spider has killed the moth, for these creatures of nature this is a perfectly fine way to begin the day. This is business as usual.)

➤ How would you paraphrase the lines "What had that flower to do with being white / The wayside blue and innocent heal-all?" (Frost is reflecting upon the innocence of the heal-all, although it served as the site for this murder of the moth.)

➤ Why do you think Frost titled this poem "Design" rather than "The Demise of a Moth" or "The Heal-all"? (The title tells the reader that the poem is about the design behind the smallest events in nature.)

Writing

QUICK ASSESS
Do students' emulations:

✓ follow Frost's sentence structure?

✓ repeat only a few of Frost's words?

✓ reflect on the chosen subject?

Students are asked to write a word-for-word emulation of Frost's sonnet "Design." Before they begin to work on their own, model how this should be done on the board or on an overhead.

READING AND WRITING EXTENSIONS

➤ Have students read the Robert Frost poem "Acquainted with the Night" and discuss how the words "One luminary clock against the sky / Proclaimed the time was neither wrong nor right" compare with the message of "Design."

➤ Ask students to bring pictures or sketches of flower and insect specimens to class. Have them make a list of philosophical questions that these aspects of nature inspire.

Four Writing a Parallel Poem

Critical Reading

FOCUS

William Stafford has said that "Writers may not be special—sensitive or talented in any usual sense. They are simply engaged in sustained use of a language skill we all have."

BACKGROUND

In *Writing the Australian Crawl*, William Stafford explains, "A writer is not so much someone who has something to say as he is someone who has found a process that will bring about new things he would not have thought of if he had not started to say them. That is, he does not draw on a reservoir; instead, he engages in an activity that brings to him a whole succession of unforeseen stories, poems, and plays."

➤ In his poem "Traveling Through the Dark," Stafford recalls a night when he found a dead deer on the road. Thinking of other drivers who might swerve and cause an accident, he stops to roll it into the canyon. As he drags her to the edge he notices that the doe is pregnant and that the fawn is still alive in her womb: "I thought hard for us all—my only swerving— / then pushed her over the edge into the river."

FOR DISCUSSION AND REFLECTION

➤ In order to make the events in this poem clear to students, ask them to sketch what is happening in each stanza.

➤ What do you think the speaker is suggesting when he says that "around our group I could hear the wilderness listen"? (Many answers are possible but are likely to include reference to the speaker's awareness of himself, the dead doe and the fawn as "a group," existentially connected by this moment, and that his decision about what to do next mattered. Nature was waiting for him to respond.)

➤ What would you have done in the speaker's place? (Answers will vary. Encourage students to explain why they would have behaved this way had they been "Traveling Through the Dark.")

Writing

QUICK ASSESS

Do students' poems:

✓ focus on a difficult decision they made?

✓ explain the possible choices and their reasoning?

✓ reflect on the significance of their choice?

Students are asked to write a parallel poem about a time when they had a difficult decision to make. Before they begin to write, have students tell their story to a partner. Answering questions the partner may have will help to flesh out the details of the story and further stimulate their memories.

READING AND WRITING EXTENSIONS

➤ Have students read Naomi Shihab Nye's poem "Bill's Beans," written upon the death of William Stafford and dedicated to the man: "He left the sky over Oregon and the fluent trees. / He gave us our lives that were hiding under our feet, / saying, You know what to do."

➤ Ask students to write a dialogue between the speaker in Stafford's poem and his wife when he returned home that evening.

Five Modeling and Drawing

C r i t i c a l   R e a d i n g

FOCUS

From Wallace Stevens's "An Ordinary Evening in New Haven":

"The eye's plain version is a thing apart."

BACKGROUND

In "Thirteen Ways of Looking at a Blackbird," Wallace Stevens offers readers thirteen different perspectives on a common blackbird. The first stanza creates a still landscape in which the "only moving thing" is the blackbird's eye. In the second stanza, Stevens plays upon the common expression "to be of two minds" and instead says that he "was of three minds" like a tree where three blackbirds perched. The third stanza pictures the blackbirds in flight, whirling "in the autumn winds." In the fourth, Stevens presents readers with the familiar paradox of a man and a woman as one and makes it new by suggesting that "A man and a woman and a blackbird / Are one." The following stanzas depict various scenes in which blackbirds are unexpectedly present. Stevens presents the reader with many imaginative challenges.

FOR DISCUSSION AND REFLECTION

➤ Have students choose a stanza that puzzled them and then read their choices to classmates. Invite other students to offer possible interpretations of the stanza.

➤ Why do you think Stevens chose such an ordinary creature as a blackbird as his subject? (Stevens uses this poem to demonstrate that even something as simple as a blackbird can trigger complex images and associations.)

➤ What picture does Stevens create in your mind with the line "It was evening all afternoon"? (This was the kind of day with heavy skies in which the sun never broke through the clouds and darkness seemed just about to fall.)

W r i t i n g

QUICK ASSESS

Do students' writings:

✓ focus on a concrete object?

✓ include five stanzas and five pictures?

Students are asked to write and illustrate a poem modeled after "Thirteen Ways of Looking at a Blackbird" using an object of their own choice. Encourage students to borrow structures or phrasings from Stevens's poem, as David Ives has done in "Thirteen Ways of Looking At a Thunderbird": "I do not know which to prefer, / The beauty of innuendoes / Or the genuine leather upholstery."

READING AND WRITING EXTENSIONS

➤ Have students choose one of the stanzas from Stevens's poems that particularly strikes them for its poignancy and write for fifteen minutes about the ideas and associations these words suggest.

➤ Have students read Henry Louis Gates's *Thirteen Ways of Looking at a Black Man*, a collection of essays exploring what it means to be a male African American in twentieth-century America. Ask them to report on why they think Gates chose this reference to Wallace Stevens's poem for his title.

Unit Overview

"The Craft of Poetry" helps students understand how poets choose the rhyme, rhythm, and form they want to use and how those elements affect the readers' experience of their poems. As they examine four poems and learn about organic form, villanelles, meter, and rhyme schemes, students will increase their abilities to understand—and enjoy—poetry.

Literature Focus

Lesson	Literature
1. Organic Poetry	**A. R. Ammons,** "Poetics" (Poetry)
2. Reading Well	**Elizabeth Bishop,** "One Art" (Poetry)
3. Crafting a Villanelle	**Theodore Roethke,** "The Waking" (Poetry)
4. Freeing the Verse Form	**Linda Pastan,** "Prosody 101" (Poetry)
5. The Idea of Poetry	

Reading Focus

1. Organic form arises from a poet's attempt to record nature and experiences as naturally as possible.

2. Good readers of poetry rely on their intelligence, intuition, and a dictionary. Nothing else is necessary to enjoy poetry.

3. The villanelle has a tightly controlled form that enables poets to use repetition to build up ideas and emotions. By the last stanza, the two repeating lines mean more than they did at the beginning.

4. The rhythm is one of a poet's most important tools for interesting the reader and emphasizing meaning.

5. Exploring the form and idea of poetry helps you become a more observant and aware reader. It also helps you appreciate the greatness of some poets' art.

Writing Focus

1. Consider the organic form of a poem.

2. Explain a poem's meaning.

3. Compose a villanelle based on a model.

4. Write about how two subjects—poetry and love—are discussed in the same poem.

5. Write a poem that includes an original definition of poetry.

One Organic Poetry

Critical Reading

FOCUS

A. R. Ammons on his creative process:

"My predisposition is to prefer confusion to over-simplified clarity, meaninglessness to neat, precise meaning, uselessness to over-directed usefulness."

BACKGROUND

A. R. Ammons (born 1926) has written that "A poem is a walk." His poetry shows a natural movement, as in "Poetics," and tends to be part Romantic and part Transcendental. Explaining this approach to poetry, Ammons has said: "The mind can exist in all kinds of ways. It can be too rigid, it can be loose to the point of lunacy, it can be disoriented, disconcerted, and so on. . . . It seems to me that in teaching, beginning with images, or rhythms, perhaps going through several motions, situations or strategies within a poem, one might gradually be lifting the students into the kind of comprehensive attention that would enable him to move into a desirable state of being, where there is complicated, free (though directed) functioning of his energy. . . . To rehearse, to alert, to freshen, to awaken the energies, not to lunacy and meaningless motion, but to concentration and focus. That is the desirable state to which art should bring you. . . ."

FOR DISCUSSION AND REFLECTION

➤ What do you think Ammons means when he says that he looks "for the way / things will turn / out spiraling from a center, / the shape / things will take to come forth in"? (Answers should include the idea that Ammons lets the subject of his poetry define the form rather than the other way around. Further evidence for this can be found in the lines "I look for the forms / things want to come as . . . .")

➤ Do you think other artists, for example painters and musicians, work this way? (Responses will vary.)

➤ What is Ammons referring to when he speaks in the final lines of a shape "that may be / summoning itself / through me / from the self not mine but ours"? (Many responses are possible but will likely include references to a collective unconscious as a source of creativity.)

Writing

QUICK ASSESS

Do students' responses:

✓ show understanding of organic form?

✓ explain what they think Ammons is trying to express?

Students are asked to explain what they think Ammons is trying to express in "Poetics." Some students might find it helpful to attempt to draw images for the ideas in the poem before they begin to write.

READING AND WRITING EXTENSIONS

➤ Have students read Denise Levertov's poem "The Dog of Art" and discuss how the poem comments on creativity and the purposes of art.

➤ Have students describe their own process for generating creative ideas for poems, stories, music, or drawings.

Two Reading Well

Critical Reading

FOCUS

Paul Fussell on meter:

"The pleasure which universally results from foot tapping and musical time-beating suggests that the pleasures of meter are essentially physical and as intimately connected with the rhythmic quality of our total experience as the similarly alternating and recurring phenomena of breathing and walking."

BACKGROUND

Many traditional forms in poetry go back to love poetry of the Middle Ages and Renaissance. Fixed form then did not mean unnatural or insincere, but artfully done, finely crafted, pleasing to the eye and ear. One such artfully crafted form is the villanelle. Originally a song in a country setting, a villanelle uses intermeshing rhymes in three-line stanzas (tercets), until the poem slows down and comes to a halt in the final four-line stanza (a quatrain).

➤ In "One Art," Elizabeth Bishop has crafted a villanelle that is both playful and serious in its definition of the art of losing. She begins by describing the familiar experience of losing keys and watches, forgetting names. In the fifth paragraph, she employs exaggeration in her description of losing cities and rivers, a continent. In the final stanza, Bishop gets to the thing she has lost that has inspired this diatribe on losing—her lover.

FOR DISCUSSION AND REFLECTION

➤ "One Art" is both a playful and serious poem. Where has Bishop made you smile? Where do you think she is saying something serious? (Answers should point to the final stanza as the place where Bishop reveals what it is that she cares very much about losing.)

➤ How does Bishop's use of a refrain affect you as a reader? (The repetition emphasizes the poem's musicality. The repeated reference to losses that are not a disaster prepare the reader for the one that is.)

➤ Why do you think the narrator advocates mastery of the art of losing? (Many answers are possible but will probably include discussion of how the speaker urges us to become experienced at leaving things behind because one day we may lose someone we love and need the practice.)

Writing

QUICK ASSESS

Do students' writings:

✓ comment on patterns of repetition?

✓ explain what they think Bishop is saying in the poem?

Students are asked to explain what they think Elizabeth Bishop is saying in "One Art." Make a list on the board of all the things she describes losing in the poem and then rank them in terms of their significance to the narrator.

READING AND WRITING EXTENSIONS

➤ Have students write about a time when they lost something that meant a great deal to them. Title it "The Art of Losing."

➤ Have students read Emily Dickinson's poem "Heart, we will forget him!" and ask them to compare this speaker's method of coping with the loss of a loved one with that of Bishop in "One Art."

Three Crafting a Villanelle

Critical Reading

FOCUS

The rhyme and rhythm pattern of a villanelle is elaborately controlled.

BACKGROUND

A formal villanelle is a nineteen-line poem composed of five tercets and a concluding quatrain, with the rhyme scheme aba, aba, aba, aba, aba, abaa. Two of the lines are repeated as follows: line 1 appears as lines 6, 12, and 18, and line 3 appears as lines 9, 15, and 19. The final quatrain concludes by repeating both line 1 and line 3. This pattern may seem unnecessarily arbitrary and mechanical, but the result is the very opposite in the hands of skilled poets such as Elizabeth Bishop in "One Art" and Theodore Roethke in "The Waking."

➤ The poem is full of paradoxes, apparently self-contradictory statements, the underlying meaning of which is revealed only by careful scrutiny. The purpose of a paradox is to arrest attention and provoke fresh thought. The statement "Less is more" is an example.

FOR DISCUSSION AND REFLECTION

➤ How is it possible to "think by feeling"? (Many responses are possible. Understanding can come from experience and emotion, as well as by intellectual effort. Roethke urges the reader to "take the lively air, / And, lovely, learn by going where to go.")

➤ Discuss the various paradoxes in the poem: "I wake to sleep," "dance from ear to ear," "This shaking keeps me steady." What do these phrases say to you? (Roethke suggests that waking to life will require embracing apparently contradictory aspects of the world. Rather than excluding those things we cannot comprehend, he enjoins us to follow his refrain.)

➤ How do you think the structural formality and repeated lines contribute to the effect of the poem? (Answers will vary but should prompt discussion of how the poem is full of seeming contradictions and paradoxes. The formal structure offers readers a stable base from which to examine them.)

Writing

QUICK ASSESS

Do students' villanelles:

✓ focus on a general subject?

✓ follow the rhyme and rhythm patterns?

Students are asked to write a villanelle of their own. Allow students to help one another as they craft the two sentences that will be their repeated lines. It may also help students if you put the pattern for rhyme and repeated lines on the board for them to follow.

READING AND WRITING EXTENSIONS

➤ Have students read Donald Justice's "Villanelle at Sundown" and compare his repeated line "I'll never be able to tell you" with Roethke's "I learn by going where I have to go." How do these lines set the tone for each of the poems?

➤ Ask students to describe their own process of waking up in the morning. Is their waking slow or sudden, painful or pleasurable?

Four Freeing the Verse Form

Critical Reading

FOCUS

A poem's rhythm often helps clarify its meaning.

BACKGROUND

In "Prosody 101," Linda Pastan recalls how she was taught that what mattered most in poetry was not a rigid adherence to form but that variations in a line could produce tension and surprise. She understood the lesson, at least as well as she, as a college student, could, but later came to understand more fully what her teacher had meant. Looking out into her garden, where a sudden cold front had taken "camellias blowsy with middle age" and surprised them with the wildness of a Maryland spring, she remembers the time her lover surprised her. She had gone to him to say "goodbye for good" but was so startled by his exuberant greeting that she could not continue as planned. At that moment she understood fully what variation in a line of poetry could do.

FOR DISCUSSION AND REFLECTION

➤ How would you paraphrase the phrase "strict iambic line goose-stepping"? What do you think her college instructor was trying to teach her about this kind of poetry? (The phrase describes poetry which adheres to form for the sake of form rather than in the service of meaning.)

➤ What does the speaker's comparison of herself with the camellias reveal to the reader? (She, like the flowers, is "blowsy with middle age" and so all the more taken aback by her lover's wildly demonstrative act of affection.)

➤ What do you think the pronoun *this* refers to in the final line? (Answers will vary but should include comparison of the sudden tension and surprise she felt at her lover's impulsive action with the effect of variation and tension in a line of carefully crafted poetry.)

Writing

QUICK ASSESS

Do students' responses:

✓ reflect a thoughtful reading of the poem?

✓ explain their decision for the placement of "Prosody 101" in an anthology?

Students are asked to decide whether they would place "Prosody 101" in the section of an anthology on love or on poems about poetry. Bring in several poetry anthologies and show students how poems are typically arranged and sorted.

READING AND WRITING EXTENSIONS

➤ Read to students from Mary Oliver's book *Rules for the Dance, A Handbook for Writing and Reading Metrical Verse* and compare Oliver's attitude towards studying form with that of Linda Pastan as portrayed in "Prosody 101."

➤ In *The San Francisco Review of Books*, Linda Pastan was described as a seer, "returning to the role of the poet as it served the human race for centuries: to fuel our thinking, show us our world in new ways, and to get us to feel more intensely." Ask students to discuss how "Prosody 101" does or doesn't "fuel" their thinking.

Five The Idea of Poetry

C r i t i c a l   R e a d i n g

FOCUS

Laurence Perrine describes poetry as "an organism whose every part serves a useful purpose and cooperates with every other part to preserve and express the life that is within it."

BACKGROUND

In *Sound and Sense*, Laurence Perrine wrote, "Poetry is as universal as language and almost as ancient. In all ages, and in all countries, poetry has been written—and eagerly read or listened to—by all kinds and conditions of people, by soldiers, statesmen, lawyers, farmers, doctors, scientists, clergy, philosophers, kings, and queens. In all ages it has been especially the concern of the educated, the intelligent, and the sensitive, and it has appealed, in its simpler forms, to the uneducated and to children. Why? First, because it has given pleasure. People have read it, listened to it, or recited it because they liked it and because it gave them enjoyment. But this is not the whole answer. Poetry in all ages has been regarded as important, not simply as one of the alternative forms of amusement, as one person might choose bowling, another chess, and another poetry. Rather, it has been regarded as something central to existence, something having unique value to the fully realized life, something that we are better off for having and spiritually impoverished without."

FOR DISCUSSION AND REFLECTION

➤ Why do you think people have always been more successful at appreciating poetry than at defining it? (Answers will vary. Help students see the difficulty of pinning down any art form to a simple definition.)

➤ What are the key features of poetry that you think should be included in any definition? (Responses will vary. Chart all student responses on the board, including those that may seem at first contradictory—for example, "It rhymes. It doesn't rhyme."

➤ Why do you think it is important to attempt to define poetry for yourself? (Many answers are possible. Students should discuss how creating a personal definition helps a reader to understand his or her own responses to poetry.)

W r i t i n g

QUICK ASSESS

Do students' poems:

✓ formulate a personal definition of poetry?

✓ illustrate their definition with concrete images?

Students are asked to write a poem that contains their own personal definition of poetry. It may help students to write out this definition first in general terms, as a dictionary might, and then illustrate this definition with particular details and concrete images from their own experience.

READING AND WRITING EXTENSIONS

➤ Have students read Lawrence Ferlinghetti's "Constantly Risking Absurdity" and discuss how a poet is constantly risking absurdity whenever he or she offers a poem to the world.

➤ Ask students to write a poem in which they define another art form such as ballet, computer programming, break dancing, sculpture, or rap music. (Allow them considerable freedom to decide what activities are art forms.)

Unit Overview

In this unit, students are invited to examine the life and writings of one of today's most popular African American writers, Toni Morrison. As they read and respond to excerpts from several of her works, they will begin to appreciate Morrison's talents as a storyteller interested in her African American heritage, a social commentator eager to expose and explore controversial issues, and a skillful writer able to juggle multiple stories and points of view in a single scene.

Literature Focus

Lesson	Literature
1. The Importance of Story	from The Nobel Prize Lecture (Nonfiction)
2. The Storyteller's Descriptions	from *The Bluest Eye* (Novel)
3. Writer as Social Commentator	
4. Structuring an Episode	from *Song of Solomon* (Novel)
5. Structuring Your Own Episode	

Reading Focus

1. A story can show the way a writer interprets the world.

2. Writers' descriptions of particular objects, characters, or events may lead a reader to see symbolic meaning beyond the particular details.

3. Many writers create their stories to explore social issues. The stories are entertaining and compelling, but they also comment on the way we live.

4. In order to reflect how we experience things, writers sometimes create scenes that tell several stories simultaneously.

5. Combining different facets of experience—thought, action, and multiple points of view—is one way of structuring an episode to bring immediacy to the scene.

Writing Focus

1. Retell a story and explain the knowledge it gave you.
2. Describe a physical feature that symbolizes your character or personality.
3. Explore the social commentary in an excerpt from a novel.
4. Identify and explain the multiple stories in a scene from a novel.
5. Write a short scene, combining the stories of three characters.

One The Importance of Story

C r i t i c a l   R e a d i n g

FOCUS

In awarding Toni Morrison the Nobel Prize in 1993, the committee said, "She delves into the language itself, a language she wants to liberate from the fetters of racism."

BACKGROUND

Toni Morrison (born 1931) was the eighth American writer to win the Nobel Prize in Literature. Born Chloe Anthony Wofford, she grew up in Lorain, Ohio, an industrial town on Lake Erie. *The Bluest Eye* (1970), her first novel, is set mostly in Lorain, which is important because Morrison's literature attempts to "escape from stereotyped black settings," a reference to earlier novels set on a plantation or in a ghetto. Growing up, Morrison was influenced by her parents, Ramah Willis and George Wofford, who had migrated from the South and who instilled a strength and pride in her. She attended Howard University (where she changed her name to Toni because people had a hard time pronouncing Chloe) and earned her masters in literature from Cornell. After college, she married, taught for a time, and worked as an editor at Random House. With the publication of *The Bluest Eye* she helped change the landscape of contemporary fiction by focusing on characters who are not only African American but African American women.

FOR DISCUSSION AND REFLECTION

➤ Why do you think Morrison chose to tell a story for her lecture? (Many responses are possible. Morrison considers herself first and foremost a storyteller and believes in the power of stories to teach.)

➤ What do you think the old woman meant when she told the young visitors "'I don't know whether the bird you are holding is dead or alive, but what I do know is that it is in your hands. It is in your hands.'"? (The young people who sought to trick her are themselves tricked by the old woman's wisdom. Whatever happens or has happened to the bird is their doing. They will forever bear responsibility for the deed.)

➤ From what Morrison says in this speech about storytelling, what do you think the stories she writes are like? (Answers should include discussion of the fact that they will reflect the oral tradition and African American heritage.)

W r i t i n g

QUICK ASSESS

Do students' writings:

✓ retell a story that meant a great deal to them?

✓ explain what they learned from this story?

Students are asked to select a story that has been important to them, retell it, and then write about the knowledge they gained from the story. It may be difficult for students to come up with a range of stories to choose from. Brainstorm on the board all the stories from folklore, mythology, and family tradition that students can remember.

READING AND WRITING EXTENSIONS

➤ Have students read John Steinbeck's 1963 Nobel Prize Lecture and compare this American storyteller's message with that of Morrison.

➤ Have students rewrite their stories for a different audience, young children perhaps.

Two The Storyteller's Descriptions

Critical Reading

FOCUS

Symbols often show connections between the physical world and the world of the mind or spirit.

BACKGROUND

Although Toni Morrison drew on many memories in writing *The Bluest Eye*, the novel is very much a work of her own imagination. Exploring the world of African American girls growing up in Depression-era Ohio, Morrison infused each of her characters with aspects of her own personality, and in so doing, embarked on a voyage of self-discovery. "All of those people were me," Morrison has said. "I was Pecola, Claudia, everybody. And as I began to write, I began to pick up scraps of things that I had seen or felt, or didn't see or feel, but imagined. And I fell in love with myself. I reclaimed myself and the world—a real revelation. I named it. I described it. I listed it. I identified it. I recreated it."

➤ Writing *The Bluest Eye*, Toni Morrison was fully convinced that "no one is ever going to read this until I'm dead." But she realized that even if the book was never published, the act of writing had unlocked "a very special place" inside her and that her life would never be the same again.

FOR DISCUSSION AND REFLECTION

➤ How does reading about Pecola make you feel? (Answers may include a discussion of how readers feel sorry for Pecola and sad that she feels ugly. "Long hours she sat looking in the mirror, trying to discover the secret of the ugliness, the ugliness that made her ignored or despised at school, by teachers and classmates alike." Students are likely to wonder what could have happened to make Pecola feel this way about herself.)

➤ What does Pecola see in the dandelions that others seem to miss? (She sees beauty and strength in their profusion where others see only weeds or greens.)

Writing

QUICK ASSESS

Do students' descriptions:

✓ focus on a physical feature of theirs?

✓ suggest how they have been defined by this feature?

✓ reveal how description can suggest symbolic meaning?

Students are asked to describe a physical feature of their own that symbolizes some aspect of their personality or character. Let students know that they are not limited to facial features but may choose to write about a special goal-kicking foot or an annoying ache in their back.

READING AND WRITING EXTENSIONS

➤ Have students read *The Bluest Eye* and explore how the imagery of eyes is developed throughout the novel.

➤ Ask students to think about a time they remember when a child was excluded and tormented by classmates the way Pecola is in the excerpt. Have them write an interior monologue for this child as he or she sits alone in the classroom.

Three Writer as Social Commentator

Critical Reading

FOCUS

Toni Morrison has said that "The impetus for writing *The Bluest Eye* was to write a book about a kind of person that was never in literature anywhere, never taken seriously by anybody—all those peripheral little girls."

BACKGROUND

Toni Morrison is outspoken on social issues. In the spring of 1993, she appeared for an interview on *The Charlie Rose Show*, a nationally televised public television program. Rose asked Morrison, if with her status as a prize-winning author and an Ivy League academic, she still had encounters with racism. "Yes, I do, Charlie," she answered, "but, let me tell you, that's the wrong question. What you should be asking is how do you feel. If you can only be tall because somebody is on their knees, then you have a serious problem. Don't you understand that the people who do this thing, who practice racism, are bereft? There is something distorted about the psyche. And racism has just as much of a deleterious effect on white people as it does on black people."

FOR DISCUSSION AND REFLECTION

➤ In the first quotation, Morrison explains that she wrote *The Bluest Eye* for all the Pecolas in the world. Do you think it is important for readers to be able to find themselves in books? (Have students support their various answers with examples from their own reading.)

➤ Why does Morrison think it would have been awful if her friend had had her prayers answered and had gotten her blue eyes? (Many answers are possible, but students should discuss how Morrison's friend's desire for blue eyes represents a deep dissatisfaction with who she really is.)

➤ How is the concept of a "bluest eye" itself a social issue? (Society determines what is beautiful and, therefore, who is valuable. By making readers empathize with Pecola, she demonstrates the injustice that is done to those without that "bluest eye.")

Writing

QUICK ASSESS

Do students' responses:

✓ mention social issues in the excerpt from *The Bluest Eye*?

✓ discuss the novel's title?

✓ explore the effect of these issues on them?

Students are asked to write about the social issues that are introduced in the excerpt from *The Bluest Eye*. Students will write most effectively if they use issues from the story that genuinely matter to them.

READING AND WRITING EXTENSIONS

➤ Have students read from Toni Morrison's *Playing in the Dark: Whiteness and the Literary Imagination*. In this series of lectures, Morrison ponders the effect that living in a racially divided society has had on American writing.

➤ Invite students to take one of the social issues that they have written about and recast it as a letter to the editor of a local newspaper. Encourage students to mail these letters.

Four Structuring an Episode

Critical Reading

FOCUS

Toni Morrison has explained that "To make the story appear oral, meandering, effortless, spoken—to have the reader feel the narrator without identifying that narrator, or hearing him or her knock about, and to have the reader work with the author in the construction of the book—is what's important."

BACKGROUND

In her essay "Thoughts on the African-American Novel," Toni Morrison has written, "I don't regard Black literature as simply books written by Black people, or simply as literature written about Black people, or simply as literature that uses a certain mode of language in which you just sort of drop g's. There is something very special and very identifiable about it and it is my struggle to find that elusive but identifiable style in the books. My joy is when I think that I have approached it; my misery is when I think I can't get there."

➤ The myth of the flying Africans was something Morrison had heard about throughout her childhood. Many slave narratives talk of blacks who could fly, and there is a famous African American folktale about a group of African-born slaves who rise up from the plantation and fly back home across the ocean. Asked about this legend after *Song of Solomon* was published, Morrison told an interviewer that, although there are parallels to the famous Greek myth about Icarus, the meaning she intended in her novel was very specific to the African American experience.

FOR DISCUSSION AND REFLECTION

➤ What aspects of this excerpt intrigue you? (Push students to explain their different answers with evidence from the text.)

➤ Why do you think people felt ambivalent toward Mr. Smith? (As their insurance man, he was a necessary part of their lives yet a constant annoyance and reminder of both their poverty and their mortality.)

➤ Why do crowds gather when someone threatens to jump from a tall building or bridge? (Answers are likely to include discussion of a natural fascination with disaster and a wonderment that someone would willingly throw his or her life away.)

Writing

QUICK ASSESS

Do students' charts:

✓ identify the separate stories?

✓ include details about each story?

Students are asked to chart the separate stories that they find in this opening to Toni Morrison's novel *Song of Solomon*. Reassure students that rereading the passage is a way to understand what is occurring in the six distinct stories. Also remind them that there is much that they cannot possibly understand about the characters from reading only this short excerpt.

READING AND WRITING EXTENSIONS

➤ Ask students to write an interior monologue for Mr. Smith. What is going through his head just before he decides to fly?

➤ Have students read *The Women of Brewster Place* by Gloria Naylor, another contemporary African American writer who uses multiple voices to tell a story. Encourage students to compare her approach with that of Toni Morrison.

Five Structuring Your Own Episode

Critical Reading

FOCUS

Toni Cade Bambara—whose literary career Toni Morrison helped develop while an editor at Random House—on Morrison's work:

"She lures you in, locks the doors and encloses you in a special, very particular universe—all in the first three pages."

BACKGROUND

In an interview in *The New Republic*, Toni Morrison made the following comment about universality in literature: "I never asked Tolstoy to write for me, a little colored girl in Lorain, Ohio. I never asked Joyce not to mention Catholicism or the world of Dublin. Never. And I don't know why I should be asked to explain your life to you. We have splendid writers to do that, but I am not one of them. It is that business of being universal, a word hopelessly stripped of meaning for me. Faulkner wrote what I suppose could be called regional literature and had it published all over the world. That's what I wish to do. If I tried to write a universal novel, it would be water. Behind this question is the suggestion that to write for black people is somehow to diminish the writing. From my perspective there are only black people. When I say 'people,' that's what I mean."

FOR DISCUSSION AND REFLECTION

➤ How does having a story told from various points of view affect you? (This method of storytelling may pose challenges to understanding; it offers a greater range of knowledge about what is happening than a more circumscribed point of view offers.)

➤ Ask students to identify places in the opening pages from *Song of Solomon* where they felt lost. (As students read these passages aloud, invite other students to share the meanings that they were able to make of them.)

➤ If you were to describe Toni Morrison's style to a friend who had never read her work, what would you say? (Answers may include her keen ear for dialogue, her poetic images, her use of concrete detail and rich imagery. Have students support their responses with evidence from various selections.)

Writing

QUICK ASSESS

Do students' scenes:

✓ change point of view while maintaining a sense of unity?

✓ interweave the stories of three different characters?

Students are asked to write a short scene in which they interweave the stories of three characters into a larger event. Encourage students to start by conceiving the larger event and then visualizing how their three different characters would interpret what was happening. Remind them that the best storytelling "shows" rather than "tells."

READING AND WRITING EXTENSIONS

➤ William Faulkner's masterpiece *The Sound and the Fury* uses multiple perspectives to tell the story. Encourage students to read this book and map the story from the different perspectives.

➤ Have students describe a time when they got in trouble with their parents—first from their own point of view, then from one parent's, and finally from that of a third person.

I n d e x

Teacher's Guide page numbers are in parentheses following pupil's edition page numbers.

L e s s o n   T i t l e   I n d e x

Literature Index